DICTI

SYNONYMS & ANTONYMS

A PERFECT REFERENCE COMPANION

— Josef S. Verghese

A TO Z DICTIONARY FOR
STUDENTS, TEACHERS & LEARNERS
OF ENGLISH LANGUAGE

MAANU
GRAPHICS

DICTIONARY OF SYNONYMS & ANTONYMS

Published by
MAANU GRAPHICS
5FF, Ganpati Bhawan, 21 Ansari Road,
Darya Ganj, New Delhi-110002
Ph: 65285220, 64138266
E-mail : maanugraphics@yahoo.com

Printed at
D. G. Printers, Delhi

CONTENTS

What are synonyms and antonyms?

A synonym is a word that has a similar meaning to another word. A thesaurus is a resource similar to a dictionary that helps writers to identify synonyms that they can use to make their own writing more interesting.

An antonym is a word meaning the opposite of a given word.

A

Abandon

(Transitive verb)

Synonyms: Quit, Evacuate, Relinquish, Give up, Surrender, Resign, Forgo, Discontinue, Waive, Abdicate, Leave, Discard, Desert

Antonyms: Keep, Chase, Pursue, Continue, Carry on, Remain Hunt, Prosecute, Follow, Undertake

Abash

(Transitive verb)

Synonyms: Humiliate, Humble, Debase, Degrade, Reduce, Depress, Mortify, Denigrate, Embarrass, Disconcert, Astound, Confound

Antonyms: Immodesty, Self-esteem, Self-love, Self-praise, Complacency, Smugness, Dignified, Upgrade, Exalt

Abate

(Intransitive Verb)

Synonyms: Decrease, Lessen, Moderate, Diminish, Subside, Ally, Slacken, Subdue, Alleviate, Dwindle, Ease, Grow Less, Reduce

Antonyms: Increase, Augment, Extreme, Enlarge, Extend, Dilate, Sprout, Expand, Swell, Grow, Advance, Develop, Rise, Ascend, Enhance, Deepen, Heighten, Intensify, Magnify, Aggravate, Spread, Disperse, Exaggerate

Abbreviate

(Transitive Verb)

Synonyms: Condense, Contract, Abridge, Clip, Shorten,

Curtail, Truncate, Trim
Anonyms: Extend, Elongate, Lengthen, Stretch, Prolong, Protract

Abduct
(Transitive Verb)
Synonyms: Kidnap, Carry off, Steal, Spirit away
Anonyms: Deliver, Give away, Surrender

Aberration
(Abstract Noun)
Synonyms: Deviation, Variation, Distortion, Disorientation, Error
Antonyms : Truth, Sanity

Abet
(Transitive verb)
Synonyms: Encourage, Incite, Aid, Assist, Support, Instigate
Antonyms: Block, Close, Affect, Hinder, Prevent, Obstruct, Interrupt, Intercept, Restrict, Restraint, Inhibit, Prohibit

Abhor
(Transitive verb)
Synonyms: Loathe, Despise, Hate, Dislike, Detest, Abominate
Antonyms: Attachment, Yearning, Passion, Devotion, Love, Fondness, Liking, Inclination, Desire, Admiration, Affection, Infatuation, Advocating, Idolatry

Abiding
(Adjective)
Synonyms: Everlasting, Constant, Continuing, Durable, Enduring, Eternal, Immortal, Permanent, Persistent, Steadfast, Unending
Anonyms: Brief, Fleeting, Momentary, Short-lived, Temporary, Transitory, Ephemeral

Ability
(Noun)

Synonyms: Expertness, Power, Skill, Competence, Competency, Capacity, Efficiency, Capability, Aptitude, Faculty, Talented
Anonyms: Unskillfulness, Impotence, Incompetence, Weakness, Incapability

Abject
(Adjective)

Synonyms: Degraded, Contemptible, Miserable, Wretched, Base, Mean, Worthless, Groveling, Repulsive
Anonyms: Insolence, Arrogance, Haughtiness, Presumption, Pomposity, Snobbery, Domineering, Defiance

Abjure
(Transitive verb)

Synonyms: Forswear, Renounce, Relinquish, Abandon, Recant, Repudiate, Renunciation
Anonyms: Desire, Like, Worship, Long for, Wish, Earn

Able
(Adjective)

Synonyms: Capable, Skilful, Learned, Accomplished, Adept, Adequate, Adroit, Clever, Competent, Efficient, Expert, Fit, Masterful, Proficient
Antonyms: Incapable, Unqualified, Impotent, Inadequate, Incompetent, Inefficient, Inept, Weak, Mediocre, Unskillful, Unfit

Abnormal
(Adjective)

Synonyms: Unusual, Aberrant, Unnatural, Eccentric, Irregular, Anomalous, Insane, Monstrous
Antonyms: Regular, Natural, Sanity, Conformity, Soundness, Reason, Rationality, Normality, Sobriety, Lucidity

Abode

(Noun)

Synonyms: Address, Domicile, House, Lodging, Residence
Antonyms: Homelessness, Addresslessness

Abolish

(Transitive verb)

Synonyms: Destroy, Suppress, Annul, Cancel, Nullify, Abrogate, Exterminate
Antonyms: Confirm, Approve, Retain, Continue, Fabricate, Build, Erect, Establish, Achieve, Complete

Abominate

(Transitive verb)

Synonyms: Hate, Abhor, Detest, Dislike, Loathe, Recoil from, Shudder at
Anonyms: Admire, Adore, Cherish, Dot on, Esteem, Love, Revere, Idolize, Worship

About

(Adjective)

Synonyms: Approximately, Nearly, Almost
Antonyms: Correctly, Accurately, Exactly, Definitely

Above

(Preposition & Adjective)

Synonyms: Over, Atop, Upon, Exceeding, Beyond, Higher than, On top of, Superior to
Antonyms: Below, Beneath, Under, Underneath, Inferior, Lesser

Above board

(Adjective)

Synonyms: Honest, Candid, Fair and square, Frank, Legitimate, Covert, Trustworthy
Antonyms: Clandestine, Deceitful, Crooked, Deceptive, Devious, Dishonest, Fraudulent, Furtive

Abridge

(Transitive Verb)

Synonyms: Shorten, Curtail, Contract, Diminish, Reduce
Antonyms: Expand, Magnify, Enlarge, Lengthen, Extent, Prolong

Abrupt

(Adjective)

Synonyms: Sudden, Hasty, Headlong, Hurried, Precipitate, Quick, Surprising, Swift, Unanticipated, Unforeseen
Antonyms: Leisurely, Slow, Thoughtful, Unhurried, Gradual

Abridgment

(Noun)

Synonyms: Abbreviation, Epitome, Summary, Abstract, Compendium, Outline, Synopsis, Analysis, Digest
Antonyms: Elaborate, Expand, Dissect, Elongate

Absence

Synonyms: Non-existence, Non-presence, Non-attendance
Antonyms: Presence, Existence, Attendance, Continuance

Abscond

(Intransitive verb)

Synonyms: Hide, Slip away, Conceal oneself, Leave, Steal away, Decamp, Retire, Depart, Retreat, Take oneself off, Disappear, Run away, Withdraw, Flee, Run off
Antonyms: Hold one's ground, Reappear, Arrive, Remain, Be present, Present one self, Come into view, Put in appearance, Stay, Emerge

Absent

(Adjective)

Synonyms: Missing, Away, Gone, Lacking, Nonexistent , Not present , Not attachment , Elsewhere
Antonyms: Attendant, Present, Alert, Attentive, Aware, Conscious

Absolute

(Adjective)

Synonyms: Arbitrary, Compulsory, Haughty, Positive, Arrogant, Controlling, Imperative, Supreme, Authoritative, Despotic, Dictatorial, Irresponsible, Unconditional, Commanding, Domineering, Over-bearing, Unequivocal, Compulsive, Exacting, Peremptory, Unlimited, imperious, tyrannical, autocratic

Antonyms: Accountable, Contingent, Lenient, Mild, Docile, Limited, Responsible, Complaint, Lowly, Submission, Conditional, Gentle, Neck, Yielding, Constitutional, humble

Absolutely

Synonyms: Entirely, Totally, Completely, Definitely, Positively, Indubitably

Antonyms: In completely, Probably, Perhaps, Partially

Absolve

(Transitive Verb)

Synonyms: Excuse, Forgive, Acquit, Clear, Deliver, Discharge, Exempt, Pardon, Release, Remit, Shrive, Vindicate, Set free

Antonyms: Blame, Censure, Charge, Convict, Denounce, Excoriate, Reprehend, Sentence, Upbraid,

Absorb

(Transitive Verb)

Synonyms: Burn, Spend, Waste, Squander, Destroy, Exhaust, Devour, Assimilate

Antonyms: Save, Hoard, Reserve, Pressure, Husband

Abstain

(Intransitive Verb)

Synonyms: Forbear, Refrain, Desist, Withhold, Resist

Antonyms: Pursue, Adopt, Persist, Offer

Abstract
(Adjective)
Synonyms: Metaphysical, Theoretical, Abstruse, Arcane, Complex, Conceptual, Deep, Hypothetical, Indefinite, Occult, Subtle, Unpractical, Unrealistic
Antonyms: Material, Persist, Concrete, Definite, Factual, Real, Specific

Absurd
(Adjective)
Synonyms: Foolish, Stupid, Ridiculous, Irrational, Senseless, Silly
Antonyms: Logical, Sound, Rational, Sensible, Consistent, Reasonable

Abundance
(Noun)
Synonyms: Plenty, Affluence, Ampleness, Bounty, Copiousness, Plientitude, Profusion, exuberance
Antonyms: Dearth, Deficiency, Lock, Need, Paucity, Scarcity, Sparseness

Abundant
(Adjective)
Synonyms: Ample, Sufficient, Lavish
Antonyms: Scarce, Limited, Insufficient, Scanty

Abuse
(Noun)
Synonyms: Contumely, Reproach, Opprobrium, Scurrility, Invective, Misusage
Antonyms: Praise, Eulogy, Adulation, Tribute, Panegyric, Economium, Commendation

Abusive
(Adjective)
Synonyms: Insulting, Calumniating, Castigating,

Contumelious, Disparaging, Libelous, Maligning, Offensive, Scolding, Reviling, Slanderous
Antonyms: Approving, Complimentary, Eulogistic, Laudatory, Praising, Panegyric

Accept
(Verb)

Synonyms : Approve, Believe, Take, Assent, Agree, Honor, Admit, Confirm
Antonyms: Disapprove, Disbelieve, Refuse, Reject, Disagree, Non-consent

Accident
(Noun)

Synonyms: Mishap, Incident, Chance, Calamity
Antonyms: Purpose, Design, Meaning, Adventure

Accidental
(Adjective)

Synonyms: Unintentional, Adventitious, Casual, Chance, Contingent, Fortuitous, Haphazard, Incidental, Random, Uncertain
Antonyms: Intended, Intentional, Planned, Prepared, Foreseen, Expected

Accompany
(Verb)

Synonyms: Ascend, Arise, Climb, Mount, Escort, Join, Attend, Chaperon, Conduct, Convoy, Consort
Antonyms: Discard, Leave, Abandon, Come down, Dismount

Accomplish
(Verb)

Synonyms: Achieve, Attain, Complete, Conclude, Effectuate, Finish, Perform, Fulfill
Antonyms: Fail, Fall, Short, Forsake, Give up

Accumulate
(Verb)
Synonyms: Assemble, Gather, Congregate, Rally, Board, Store, Convene
Antonyms: Sprinkle, Disperse, Scatter, Broadcast, Spread, Dissipate, Distribute

Accurate
(Adjective)
Synonyms: Correct, Precise, Exact, Nice, Right, True
Antonyms: Incorrect, Inaccurate, Inexact, Wrong, False, Erroneous

Accuse
(Verb)
Synonyms: Allege, Arraign, Attribute, Blame, Censure, Cite, Denounce, Impute, Indict
Antonyms: Absolve, Defend, Exonerate, Vindicate

Accustomed
(Adjective)
Synonyms: Usual, Common, Conventional, Customary, Expected, Habitual, Normal, Ordinary, Regular, Routine, Adopted, Familiar
Antonyms: Abnormal, Infrequent, Occasional, Odd, Peculiar, Rare, Strange, Unusual,

Achieve
(verb)
Synonyms: Attain, Accomplish, Do, Win, Effect, Fulfill, Gain, Perform, Finish, Execute, Acquire,
Antonyms: Fail, Miss, Miscarry, Loss, Give in

Acknowledge
(Verb)
Synonyms: Grant, Give, Yield, Admit, Own, Profess, Deny, Disown, Disclaim, Avow

Antonyms: Disavow, Contradict, Foreswear, Deny, Disown, Disclaim

Across
(Adjective)
Synonyms: Crosswise, Athwart, Transversely
Antonyms: Beside, Alongside, Along, Lengthwise, Longitudinal

Acme
(Noun)
Synonyms: High point, Apex, Climax, Crest, Crown, Culmination, Optimum, Peak, Pinnacle, Top, Vertex, Zenith
Antonyms: Bottom, Depths, Low point, Minimum, Nadir, Zero

Acquaintance
(Noun)
Synonyms: Friendship, Knowledge, Information, Familiarity
Antonyms: Enmity, Ignorance, Lack of knowledge, Hostility

Acquire
(Verb)
Synonyms: Achieve, Amass, Attain, Buy, Collect, Earn, Gain, Gather, Get, Obtain, Procure, Realize, Receive, Score
Antonyms: Be deprived of, Forfeit, Forgo, Give up, Lose, Relinquish, Renounce, Surrender, Waive,

Acquit
(Verb)
Synonyms: Excuse, Clear, Absolve, Deliver, Discharge, Exculpate, Exonerate, Free, Fulfill, Release, Relieve, Vindicate
Antonyms: Accuse, Involve, Blame, Charge. Condemn, Convict, Sentence, Damn

Acrimonious
(Adjective)
Synonyms: Acerbic, Astringent, Biting, Caustic, Censorious, Churlish, Cutting, Irascible, Mordacious, Peevish, Petulant,

Pungent, Rancorous, Sarcastic, Severe, Sharp, Spiteful, Tart, Trenchant, Vitriolic
Antonyms: Affable, Benign, Forgiving, Good-tempered, Kind

Act
(Noun)
Synonyms: Perform, Work, Imitate, Show
Antonyms: Laze, Stand, Idle, Hide

Active
(Adjective)
Synonyms: Quick, Prompt, Busy, Bustling, Engaged, Hard-working, Alert, Animated, Diligent, Industrious, Nimble, Vibrant, Vigorous, Vital
Antonyms: Dormant, Dull, Idle, Inactive, Inoperative, Lazy, Slow, Sedentary, Sluggish, Torpid, Unimaginative

Actual
(Adjective)
Synonyms : Existing, True, Genuine, Authentic, Real, Certain, Demonstrable
Antonyms : Uncertain, Potential, Fabulous, Virtual, Unreal

Acute
(Adjective)
Synonyms: Serious, Critical, Crucial, Grave, Decisive, Important, Severe, Urgent, Vital
Antonyms : Dense, Dim, Dim-witted, Dull, Obtuse, Slow, Stupid, Unintelligent

Adamant
(Adjective)
Synonyms : Firm, Fixed, Immovable, Inexorable, Inflexible, Insistent, Intransigent, Obdurate, Relentless, Resolute, Rigid, Stiff, Stubborn, Unbending, Uncompromising, Unshakable, Obstinate
Antonyms : Compliant, Compromising, Easy-going, Flexible, Lax, Pliant, Receptive, Responsive, Susceptible

Adapt
(Verb)

Synonyms : Fit, Regulate, Conform, Suit
Antonyms : Misfit, Irregularities, Differ, Disagree

Address
(Verb)

Synonyms : Speak to, Accost, Court, Woo, Greet, Salute, Hail, Appeal to
Antonyms : Ignore, Neglect, Pass by, Overlook, Disregard, Skip

Adjust
(Verb)

Synonyms: Set in order, Arrange, Set right, Regulate, Accommodate, Settle, Set, Compose
Antonyms: Displace, Disarrange, Dislocate, Disconnect, Derange, Disjoint

Admiration
(Noun)

Synonyms: Love, Regard, Respect, Praise
Antonyms: Hate, Disregard, Disapproval

Admire
(Verb)

Synonyms: Applaud, Extol, Approve, Praise
Antonyms: Despise, Blame, Condemn, Disapprove

Admit
(Verb)

Synonyms: Own, Avow, Grant, Concede, Give, Yield
Antonyms: Disown, Disavow, Deny, Dispute, Disclaim

Adopt
(Verb)

Synonyms: Accept, Appropriate, Approve, Assume, Embrace, Endorse, Espouse, Follow, Maintain, Ratify, Sleet, Support

Antonyms: Abandon, Abnegate, Cast aside, Cast off, Disclaim, Disown, Give up, Reject, Renounce, Repudiate, Spurn

Adore

(Verb)

Synonyms: Admire, Bow to, Cherish, Dote on, Esteem, Exalt, Glorify, Honor, Idolize, Revere, Venerate, Worship

Antonyms: Abhor, Abominate, Despise, Detest, Execrate, Hate, Loathe

Advance

(Verb)

Synonyms: Forward, Progress, Proceed, Further, Go

Antonyms: Go backward, Berid, Regress, Recede

Advantage

(Noun)

Synonyms: Utility, Emolument, Superiority, Avail, Gain, Profit, Benefit, Service

Antonyms: Obstruction, Check, Hindrance, Restraint, Impediment

Adversity

(Noun)

Synonyms: Affliction, Misery, Poverty, Misfortune

Antonyms: Prosperity, Lick, Fortune, Happiness, Progress

Advise

(Verb)

Synonyms: Warn, Admonish, Recommend, Counsel, Suggest, Prompt

Antonyms: Deter, Dissuade, Restrain, Hinder, Discourage, Criticize

Affable

(Adjective)

Synonyms: Amiable, Amicable, Benevolent, Benign, Congenial, Cordially, Courteous, Genial, Gracious, Mild,

Pleasant, Sociable
Antonyms: Brusque, Cold, Discourteous, Distant, Haughty, Ride, Surly, Unfriendly, Ungracious, Unpleasant

Affecting

(Adjective)

Synonyms: Touching, Melting, Moving, Pathetic, Eloquent, Impressive, Changing
Antonyms: Amusing, Droll, Ridiculous, Absurd, Funny, Comic, Laughable, Farcical.

Affection

(Noun)

Synonyms: Fondness, Tenderness, Attachment, Kindness, Liking, Passion, Love, Devotion, Endearment, Feeling
Antonyms: Coolness, Coldness, Negligence, Carelessness, Unconcern, Dislike, Indifference, Apathy.

Afraid

(Adjective)

Synonyms: Frightened, Scared, Fearful, Panicky, Fainthearted, Anxious
Antonyms: Brave, Bold, Courageous, Unafraid, Daring, Upright

Age

(Noun)

Synonyms: Date, Time, Period, Generation
Antonyms: Eternity, Perpetuity, Ceaselessness, Endlessness

Agent

(Noun)

Synonyms: Proxy, Delegate, Deputy, Representative, Substitute, Factor, Middleman
Antonyms: Antagonist, Opponent, Competitor, Opposer, Rival

Agony
(Noun)

Synonyms: Ache, Woe, Anguish
Antonyms: Comfort, Peace, Relief, Ease, Enjoyment

Agree
(Verb)

Synonyms: Conform, Concur, Comply, Accede, Coincide, Tally, Consent
Antonyms: Vary, Dissent, Deviate, Diverge, Differ, Refuse, Disagree, Dispute

Agreeable
(Adjective)

Synonyms: Pleasant, Gratifying, Pleasing, Acceptable, Pleasurable, Welcome, Good, Delicious
Antonyms: Offensive, Nasty, Unpleasant, Unacceptable, Disgusting, Hateful, Objectionable

Agreement
(Adjective)

Synonyms: Unison, Coincidence, Consonance, Harmony, Concurrence, Unanimity, Accordance, Concord
Antonyms: Difference, Contention, Variance, Strife, Discord, Dispute, Disagreement, Dissension

Aid
(Verb)

Synonyms: Support, Assistance, Relief, Contribute, Help, Befriend, Succour, Relieve, Co-operate, Assist, Support
Antonyms: Obstruction, Oppose, Retard, Hinder, Obstruct, Deter, Impede, Check, Hindrance

Alarm
(Noun)

Synonyms: Frighten, Startle, Appal, Terrify, Intimidate
Antonyms: Calm, Compose, Pacify, Appease, Still, Quieten

Alarming

(Adjective)

Synonyms: Frightful, Terrible, Ominous
Antonyms: Hopeful, Bright, Auspicious

Alike

(Adjective)

Synonyms: Equal, Equivalent, Resembling, Similar, Identical, Same, Allied
Antonyms: Unlike, Non-identical, Dissimilar, Different, Diverse

Allay

(Verb)

Synonyms: Ease, Lighten, Abate, Relieve, Palliate, Soothe, Rid, Assuage
Antonyms: Aggravate, Enhance, Worsen, Heighten

Allegiance

(Noun)

Synonyms: Adherence, Constancy, Devotion, Duty, Faithfulness, Fealty, Fidelity, Homage, Obedience, Obligation, Consistency
Antonyms: Disloyalty, Faithfulness, Falseness, Inconstancy, Infidelity, Perfidy, Treachery, Treason

Alliance

(Noun)

Synonyms: Affiliation, Affinity, Agreement, Association, Coalition, Combination, Compact, Concordant, Confederacy, Connection, Federation, League, Pact, Partnership, Treaty
Antonyms: Alienation, Breach, Break, Disaffection, Dissociation, Disunion, Disunity, Division, Rapture, Separation, Severance, Split

Allow

(Adjective)

Synonyms: Permit, Yield, Give, Concede, Admit Authorise, Grant, Sanction, Apportion, Assign

Antonyms: Refuse, Reject, Disavow, Renounce, Deny, Abjure, Refute, Disclaim, Withhold, Reserve

Allure

(Verb)

Synonyms: Charm, Invite, Entice, Draw, Fascinate, Endear

Antonyms: Repulse, Rebuff; Reject, Repel, Deter, Check

Ally

(Noun)

Synonyms: Friend, Accessory, Abettor, Spy, Companion, Cooperator, Colleague, Partner, Accomplice

Antonyms: Enemy, Opponent, Rival, Competitor, Opposer, Foe, Antagonist

Almighty

(Noun)

Synonyms: Absolute, All-powerful, Invincible, Omnipotent, Omnipresent, Omniscient, Supreme, Unlimited

Antonyms: Helpless, Impotent, Powerless, Weak, Feeble, Insignificant, Paltry, Poor

Almost

(Adjective)

Synonyms: About, Nearly, Towards

Antonyms: Precisely, Exactly

Alone

(Adjective)

Synonyms: Abandoned, Apart, By itself, Deserted, Desolate, Forlorn, Lonely, Single, Lone, Isolated

Antonyms: Accompanied, Aided, Among others, Assisted, Escorted, Helped, Joint, Together

Altruistic

(Adjective)

Synonyms: Benevolent, Charitable, Considerate, Generous, Humanitarian, Philanthropic, Self-sacrificing, Unselfish

Antonyms: Egoistical, Egotistical, Greedy, Mean, Self-centered, Self-interested, Selfish, Self-seeking

Always

(Adverb)

Synonyms: Continually, Uniformly, Aye, Consistently, Constantly, Eternally, Ever, Everlasting, Evermore, Forever, Invariably, Perpetually

Antonyms: Never, At no time, Hardly ever, Infrequently, Once in a blue moon, Once in a while, Only now and then, Rarely, Scarcely, Ever seldom

Amazing

(Adjective)

Synonyms: Extraordinary, Surprising, Miraculous, Marvelous, Wondrous, Stupendous, Wonderful, Astounding

Antonyms: Ordinary, Normal, Common, Everyday, Commonplace, Average, Habitual, Usual

Ambition

(Noun)

Synonyms: Purpose, Desire, Wish, Hope, Intention, Goal, End, Destination, End post, Aim

Antonyms: Indifference, Purposelessness, Aimlessness, Helplessness

Amorous

(Adjective)

Synonyms: Affectionate, Amatory, Ardent, Attached, Doting, Enamored, Erotic, Fond, Impassioned, In love, Lovesick, Lustful, Passionate, Tender, Loving

Antonyms: Aloof, Cold, Distant, Frigid, Frosty, Indifferent, Passionless, Standoffish, Undemonstrative, Unfeeling, Unloving

Amongst
(Preposition)
Synonyms: Amid, Amidst, Mid, Between
Antonyms: External, Outside, Outward, Exterior

Ample
(Adjective)
Synonyms: Full, Broad, Unrestricted, Unlimited, Sufficient, Large, Spacious, Abundant, Extensive
Antonyms: Scarce, Short, Restricted, Limited, Insufficient, Small, Skimpy, Narrow

Amuse
(Verb)
Synonyms: Please, Enliven, Entertain, Gladden, Charm, Cheer
Antonyms: Bore, Annoy, Tire, Fatigue, Wax

Ancient
(Adjective)
Synonyms: Antiquated, Aged, Old, Hoary, Antique, Venerabl
Antonyms: Fashionable, New, Young, Modern, Fresh, Green

Angel
(Noun)
Synonyms: Seraph, Cherub
Antonyms: Devil, Demon, Satan

Anger
(Noun)
Synonyms: Irritation, Fury, Resentment, Rage, Annoyance, Displease, Vex, Incite
Antonyms: Calmness, Peace, Tranquillity, Serenity, Pacify, Compose, Reconcile

Animated
(Adjective)
Synonyms: Active, Airy, Alive and kicking, Ardent, Brisk, Buoyant, Dynamic, Ebullient, Elated, Energetic, Enthusiastic,

Excited, Fervent, Gay, Passionate, Quick, Sparky, Vivacious, Vivid, Zealous, Zestful
Antonyms: Apathetic, Boring, Dejected, Depressed, Dull, Inactive, Lethargic, Lifeless, Listless, Monotonous, Passive

Animosity
(Noun)

Synonyms: Acrimony, Animus, Antagonism, Antipathy, Bad blood, Bitterness, Enmity, Hatred, Ill will, Malevolence, Malice, Rancor, Virulence, Resentment
Antonyms: Amity, Benevolence, Congeniality, Friendliness, Friendship, Goodwill, Harmony, Kindness, Love, Rapport, Sympathy

Annexation
(Noun)

Synonyms: Increase, Expansion, Supplement, Augmentation, Accession, Extension, Appendix
Antonyms: Decrease, Contraction, Curtailment, Subtraction, Diminution, Reduction, Fall

Annihilate
(Verb)

Synonyms: Destroy, Cancel, Annul, Suppress, Extinguish, Supersede, Repeal
Antonyms: Establish, Confirm, Support, Encourage, Promote, Forward, Produce, Testify

Announce
(Verb)

Synonyms: Advertise, Publish, Reveal, Declare, Notify, Proclaim, Promulgate
Antonyms: Suppress, Screen, Conceal, Withhold, Cover-up, Stifle, Subdue.

Annoy
(Verb)
Synonyms: Worry, Torment, Trouble, Vex, Irritate, Disturb, Bother, Harass, Tease
Antonyms: Please, Charm, Oblige, Gratify, Gladden, Delight

Answer
(Verb)
Synonyms: Reply, Retort, Repartee, Rejoinder, Response, Solution
Antonyms: Query, Interrogation, Defiance, Question

Antiquated
(Adjective)
Synonyms: Antediluvian, Antique, Archaic, Date, Old-fashioned, Outmoded, Out-of-date, Obsolete, Outworn, Passe, Old, Superannuated
Antonyms: Current, Fashionable, Fresh, Modern, Modish, New, Stylish, Up-to-date, Young

Anxiety
(Noun)
Synonyms: Restlessness, Apprehension, Disquiet, Dread, Worry, Misgiving, Foreboding, Uneasiness, Concern
Antonyms: Assurance, Calmness, Composure, Confidence, Ace, Security, Quietude, Equanimity

Anxious
(Adjective)
Synonyms: Troubled, Solicitous, Concerned, Earnest, Uneasy
Antonyms: Careless, Negligent, Heedless, Unmindful, Thoughtless

Aplomb
(Noun)
Synonyms: Self-possession, Balance, Calmness, Composure, Confidence, Coolness, Equanimity, Poise, Self-assurance,

Stability, Self-confidence
Antonyms: Awkwardness, Chagrin, Confusion, Discomfiture, Discomposure, Embarrassment, Self-consciousness

Apocryphal
(Adjective)
Synonyms: Doubtful, Dubious, Equivocal, Fictitious, Legendry, Mythical, Spurious, Unauthenticated, Uncanonical
Antonyms: Attested, Authentic, Authorized, Canonical, Credible,Factual, Substantiated, True, Undisputed Verified

Apparent
(Adjective)
Synonyms: Blatant, Bold, Clear, Conspicuous, Discernible, Distinct, Evident, Indubitable, Manifest, Obvious, Open, Patent, Salient, Visible, Overt
Antonyms: Ambiguous, Doubtful, Dubious, Hazy, Indefinite, Indistinct, Obscure, Uncertain, Unclear, Vague

Appearance
(Noun)
Synonyms: Phenomenon, Vista, Sight, View, Show, Outlook, Scene, Tableau, Scenery, Setting, Picture, Landscape
Antonyms: Formless, Distorted, Skeleton, Insulting

Appetite
(Noun)
Synonyms: Ambition, Desire, Hunger, Relish, Craving, Longing, Gusto
Antonyms: Realisation, Contentment, Satisfaction, Apathy

Appreciation
(Noun)
Synonyms: Love, Regard, Respect, Praise
Antonyms: Hate, Disrespect, Disregard, Condemn, Disapprove

Appropriate
(Verb)

Synonyms: Confiscate, Take, Allot, Seize, Correct
Antonyms: Release, Relinquish, Open, Loosen, Incorrect

Approve
(Verb)

Synonyms: Uphold, Acclaim, Admire, Applaud, Appreciate, Commend, Esteem, Like, Regard highly, Respect, Accept, Advocate, Allow, Confirm, Bless, Give the green signal, Mandate
Antonyms: Blame, Censure, Condemn, Deplore, Deprecate, Disapprove, Dislike, Frown upon, Object to, Disallow, Discountenance, Veto

Apt
(Adjective)

Synonyms: Suitable, Fitting, Liable, Likely, Prone, Ready, Apposite, Befitting, Correct, Germane, Meet, Pertinent, Proper, Relevant, Quick-witted
Antonyms: Ill-fitted, Improper, Inapplicable, Inapposite, Infelicitous, Irrelevant, Awkward, Clumsy, Dull, Gauche, Incompetent, Maladroit, Slow, Stupid

Arbitrary
(Adjective)

Synonyms: Capricious, Chance, Discretionary, Erratic, Fanciful, Inconsistent, Optional, Personal, Subjective, Unreasonable, Whimsical, Illogical, Irrational
Antonyms: Consistent, Judicious, Logical, Objective, Rational, Reasonable, Sensible, Sound

Archaic
(Adjective)

Synonyms: Ancient, Antique, Bygone, Olden, Primitive, Obsolete, Out of date, Passe, Superannuated
Antonyms: Contemporary, Current, Modern, New, Present,

Recent, Fresh, Latest, Novel

Argue
(Verb)
Synonyms: Debate, Discuss, Contend, Dispute, Reason, Plead
Antonyms: Concur, Acquiesce, Accede, Assent, Agree, Consent

Arrange
(Verb)
Synonyms: Put in, Array, Classify, Dispose, Group, Adjust
Antonyms: Separate, Disarrange, Scatter, Disperse, Diffuse, Disseminate

Arrest
(Verb)
Synonyms: Capture, Detain, Withhold, Stop back, Apprehend, Obstruct, Check
Antonyms: Release, Liberate, Discharge, Free, Exempt, Acquit, Unloose

Arrive
(Verb)
Synonyms: Access, Alight, Appear, Attain, Barge in, Blow in, Bob up, Breeze in, Bust in, Buzz, Check in, Clock in, Disembark, Dismount, Drop anchor, Drop in, Enter, Fall by, Fall in, Get to, Hit, Hit town, Land, Make it, Pop in, Pop Up, Pull in, Punch in, Reach, Report, Roll in, Show, Show up, Sign in, Take place, Turn up, Visit
Antonyms: Depart, Exit, Go, Leave

Ascent
(Verb)
Synonyms: Further, Go forward, Progress, Proceed
Antonyms: Bend, Go backward, Regress, Recede, Descend

Associate
(Verb)
Synonyms: Connect, Ally, Band, Fraternize, Join, Combine, Unite, Relate, Link
Antonyms: Disconnect, Separate, Defy, Break apart, Dissociate, Desert

Assure
(Verb)
Synonyms: Ensure, Guarantee, Certify, Uphold, Encourage, Promise, Inform
Antonyms: Imperil, Unsettle, Discourage, Mislead, Warn, Jeopardize

Assume
(Verb)
Synonyms: Pretend, Affect, Feign, Shame, Suppose, Imply, Presume, Presuppose, Simulate
Antonyms: Abandon, Cast-off, Discard, Reprove, Substantiate, Confirm, Establish,. Verify

Astonish
(Verb)
Synonyms: Surprise, Amaze, Astound, Startle; Confound
Antonyms: Forewarn, Caution, Warn

Attach
(Verb)
Synonyms: Unite, Link, Join, Conjoin, Couple, Combine
Antonyms: Disunite, Separate, Cut, Sever, Divide, Part, Detach, Dissever

Attract
(Verb)
Synonyms: Allure, Bewitch, Captivate, Charm, Decoy, Draw, Enchant, Endear, Engage, Entice, Fascinate, Incline, Induce, Interest, Invite, Lure, Tempt

Antonyms: Disgust, Give one the creeps, Put one off, Repel, Repulse, Revolt, Reject, Deter, Check, Rebuff, Detest

Augment
(Verb)

Synonyms: Add to, Amplify, Boost, Build up, Dilate, Enhance, Enlarge, Expand, Extend, Grow, Intensify, Magnify, Multiply
Antonyms: Contract, Curtail, Cut down, Decrease, Diminish, Lessen, Lower, Reduce, Shrink

Attention
(Noun)

Synonyms: Thoughtfulness, Mindfulness, Care, Study, Heed, Regard, Notice
Antonyms: Carelessness, Neglect, Absence, Distraction, Remission

Auspicious
(Adjective)

Synonyms: Proposition, Successful, Hopeful, Happy, Fortunate, Lucky, Reasonable
Antonyms: Despairing, Hopeless, Unhappy, Unfortunate, Unlucky, Luckless, Ill-fated

Authority
(Noun)

Synonyms: Power, Right, Title, Jurisdiction, Influence, Prestige, Control, Command, Rule, Sway
Antonyms: Submission, Obedience, Subjection, Thraldom, Slavery

Avoidance
(Noun)

Synonyms: Elusion, Retract, Abstinence, Evasion, Truant, The brush-off, The go-by, Escape, Regression
Antonyms: Continuation, Firmness, Status-quo, Pursuit, Discipline

✱

Awkward

(Adjective)

Synonyms: Unskilled, Uncouth, Rough, Ponderous, Heavy handed, Maladroit, Bungling

Antonyms: Skillful, Dexterous, Clever, Adept

B

Backward

(Adjective)

Synonyms: Posterior, Unwilling, Behind, Dull, Sluggish, Late, Tardy, Reluctant

Antonyms: Willing, Ahead, Anterior, Quick, Alert, Early, Advancing, Forward, Prompt, Eager

Baffle

(Verb)

Synonyms: Amaze, Astound, Bewilder, Confound, Confuse, Daze, Disconcert, Elude, Flummox, Mystify, Nonplus, Perplex, Stump, Stun, Balk, Defeat, Hinder, Thwart, Upset, Foil

Antonyms: Clarify, Elucidate, Explain, Explicate, Interpret, Spell out

Balance

(Verb)

Synonyms: Compensate, Estimate, Equalize, Adjust, Poise, Weight, Pit

Antonyms: Invert, Subvert, Overbalance, Tilt, Upset

Banal

(Adjective)

Synonyms: Cliched, Commonplace, Everyday, Hackneyed, Humdrum, Mundane, Ordinary, Pedestrian, State, Stereotyped, Tired, Trite, Vapid, Uninteresting

Antonyms: Challenging, Distinctive, Fresh, Imaginative, Interesting, New, Novel, Original, Stimulating, Unique Unusual

Bankrupt
(Adjective)
Synonyms: Insolvent, Penniless, Ruined, Indigent, Destitute
Antonyms: Solvent, Creditworthy, Well-off, Prosperous, Rich

Bargain
(Noun)
Synonyms: Deal, Inexpensive, Transaction, Agreement, Contract
Antonyms: Account, Closed, Expensiveness, Quittance, Payment

Barren
(Adjective)
Synonyms: Arid, Desert, Desolate, Dry, Empty, Unfruitful, Waste, Fruitless, Unsuccessful, Useless, Boring, Childless, In fecund, Sterile, Vapid, Unproductive
Antonyms: Fecund, Fertile, Fruitless, Lush, Productive, Profitable, Rich, Useless, Interesting

Base
(Adjective)
Synonyms: Corrupt, Shameful, Mean, Sordid, Low, Dishonorable, Vile
Antonyms: Aboveboard, Pure, Honored, Esteemed, Noble, Exalted, Lofty

Bashful
(Adjective)
Synonyms: Abashed, Blushing, Confused, Coy, Diffident, Easily, Embarrassed, Overmodest, Reserved, Reticent, Sheepish, Shrinking, Timid, Timorous
Antonyms: Aggressive, Arrogant, Bold, Brash, Conceited, Confident, Egoistic, Fearless, Forward, Immodest, Impudent

Bear
(Verb)
Synonyms: Support, Cherish, Entertain, Exhibit, Harbor, Have, Hold, Maintain, Possess, Shoulder, Sustain, Uphold, Bring,

Beget, Breed forth, Develop, Engender, Generate, Abide, Admit, Brook, Endure

Antonyms: Resist, Abandon, Cease, Desert, Discontinue, Drop, Give up, Leave, Quit, Relinquish, Put down, Shed

Bend

(Verb)

Synonyms: Bow, Submit, Stoop, Yield, Condescend, Lean, Tend, Incline

Antonyms: Break, Stiffen, Stand, Advance, Rise, Straighten

Before

(Preposition, Conjunction & Adverb)

Synonyms: Preceding, Ahead, Prior to, In front of, Previous to, Formerly, Above, Already

Antonyms: Succeeding, After, Behind, Alter, Following, Subsequently, Afterward

Belief

(Noun)

Synonyms: Trust, Credit, Faith, Opinion, Idea, View, Mind

Antonyms: Distrust, Whim, Discredit, Suspicion, Doubt, Disbelief, Misgiving

Beneath

(Preposition)

Synonyms: Underfoot, Below, Underneath, Under, Down, Not worthy

Antonyms:. Up, Overhead, Above, High

Benefit

(Noun)

Synonyms: Profit, Gain, Favour, Advantage, Avail, Service, Boon

Antonyms: Harm, Loss, Disadvantage, Damage, Injury, Calamity

Birth
(Noun)

Synonyms Origin, Delivery, Beginning, Creation, Genesis
Antonyms End, Finish, Close, Death, Conclusion

Bitter
(Adjective)

Synonyms Tart, Acrimonious, Acrid, Intense, Sad, Harsh, Sour, Severe
Antonyms Saccharine, Sugary, Mild, Sweet, Pleasant, Genial, Light

Blame
(Verb)

Synonyms Criticism, Reproach, Censure, Guilt, Rebuke
Antonyms Praise, Appreciation, Approval, Exhort, Applaud, Extol

Blessing
(Noun)

Synonyms Good wishes, Prayer, Thanks, Praise, Consecration
Antonyms Bad wishes, Curse, Evil thought

Bliss
(Noun)

Synonyms Joy, Pleasure, Happiness, Rapture
Antonyms Sorrow, Sadness, Pain, Dejection

Blithe
(Adjective)

Synonyms Careless, Casual, Indifferent, Nonchalant, Thoughtless, Untroubled, Animated, Buoyant, Carefree, Cheerful, Cheery, Debonair
Antonyms Concerned, Preoccupied, Thoughtful, Dejected, Depressed, Gloomy, Melancholy, Morose, Sad, Unhappy

Blunt
(Adjective)
Synonyms Direct, Insensitive, Dull, Undiplomatic
Antonyms Diplomatic, Sensitive, Sharp, Sophisticated

Boost
(Noun)
Synonyms Encouragement, Aid, Help, Recommendation, Hoist, Lift
Antonyms Rebuke, Discouragement, Hindrance, Obstacle, Rebuff

Border
(Noun)
Synonyms Edge, Brink, Limit, Margin, Boundary, Brim, Rim
Antonyms Centre, Midst, Point, Middle, Axis

Bore
(Noun)
Synonyms Troublesome, Talker, Nuisance, Talkative, Pest
Antonyms Thinker, Genial, Listener, Entertainer, Amusing

Borrow
(Verb)
Synonyms Receive, Appropriate, Take, Adapt, Adopt, Steal, Imitate, Pilfer, Pirate, Copy
Antonyms Lend, Advance, Give invent, Improve, Make, Credit

Brace
(Verb)
Synonyms Strengthen, Invigorate, Prop, Support, Refresh
Antonyms Weaken, Degenerate, Raze, Knock, Enfeeble

Brave
(Adjective)
Synonyms Fearless, Doughty, Bold, Courageous, Dauntless, Gallant, Heroic, Intrepid, Plucky, Undaunted, Valiant, Valorous
Antonyms Fearful, Afraid, Cowardly, Daunted, Timid, Intimidated, unheroic

Break

(Noun)

Synonyms Disobey, Interlude, Intermission, Interval, Letup, Full, Pause, Recess, Respite, Spell

Antonyms Obey, Comply, Repair, Continuation, Connection, Attach, Fasten, Join, Unite

Breed

(Verb)

Synonyms Produce, Raise, Beget, Conceive, Train, Hatch, Incubate

Antonyms Destroy, Slay, Murder, Annihilate, Kill

Breeze

(Noun)

Synonyms Storm, Gust, Hurricane, Wind, Typhoon, Blast, Gale

Antonyms Calm, Lull, Placidity, Doldrums

Brevity

(Noun)

Synonyms Short, Concise, Succinct, Brief

Antonyms Confused, Loquacious, Addle headed

Bright

(Adjective)

Synonyms Shining, Quick-witted, Intelligent, Luminous, Resplendent, Sparkling

Antonyms Dull, Dim, Foolish, Dark, Ignorant, Faint

Brusque

(Adjective)

Synonyms Discourteous, Gruff, Cut, Abrupt

Antonyms Courteous, Smooth, Polite, Polished

Brutal

(Adjective)

Synonyms Inhuman, Merciless, Cruel, Savage, Pitiless, Barbarous

Antonyms Tender, Humane, Merciful, Kind, Sympathetic, Compassionate

Busy
(Adjective)

Synonyms Active, Occupied, Diligent, Industrious, Engaged, Engrossed
Antonyms Indolent, Idle, Inactive, Lazy, Unoccupied, Inert, Passive, Relaxed

C

Cajole
(Verb)
Synonyms Beguile, Inveigle, Coax, Flatter, Blandish, Wheedle
Antonyms Dampen, Cool, Flaunt, Dam, Dissuade

Calamity
(Noun)
Synonyms Distress, Misfortune, Trouble, Misery, Catastrophe, Affliction, Disaster
Antonyms Prosperity, Fortune, Peace, Joy, Tranquility, Happiness

Calculate
(Verb)
Synonyms Reckon, Count, Assess, Estimate, Number, Computer
Antonyms Imagine, Conjecture, Surmise, Suppose

Call
(Verb)
Synonyms Convoke, Bid, Recall, Invite, Summon, Muster, Convent, Invoke
Antonyms Remove, Dismiss, Discharge, Exile, Banish

Calm
(Adjective)
Synonyms Pacify, Hush, Compose, Quiet, Solace, Palliate, Mitigate, Lull
Antonyms Agitate, Excite, Perturb, Crisis, Disturb, Fluster

Cancel
(Verb)

Synonyms Delete, Destroy, Abolish, Obliterate, Blot out, Efface, Nullify, Invalidate, Erase, Bite
Antonyms Establish, Ratify, Corroborate, Substantiate, Endorse, Confirm

Capacity
(Noun)

Synonyms Capability, Ability, Competence, Aptitude, Faculty, Skill, Wit, Talent, Power
Antonyms Incapability, Inability, Incompetence

Capture
(Verb)

Synonyms Arrest, Seize, Snatch, Catch, Apprehend
Antonyms Liberate, Release, Acquit, Free, Disengage

Care
(Noun)

Synonyms Carefulness, Regard, Prudence, Thrift, Wariness, Custody
Antonyms Unconcern, Coolness, Remissness, Temerity, Neglect

Careful
(Adjective)

Synonyms: Meticulous, Conscientious, Scrupulous, Punctilious
Antonyms: Negligent, Heedless, Sloppy, Slipshod

Carry
(Verb)

Synonyms: Sustain, Support, Bear, Bring, Haul, Convey, Take, Transport
Antonyms: Leave, Abandon, Drop, Let fall

Casualty
(Noun)

Synonyms: Mishap, Incident, Chance, Calamity, Misadventure

Antonyms: Design, Purpose, Intent, Meaning, Adventure

Catching
(Adjective)
Synonyms: Charming, Attractive, Appealing, Enchanting, Captivating, Winning, Fascinating
Antonyms: Unpleasant, Ugly, Unattractive, Revolting, Loathsome, Repellant, Odious, Disagreeable

Cause
(Verb)
Synonyms: Produce, Bring about, Originate, Evoke, Create, Effect
Antonyms: Destroy, Demolish, Kill, Devastate, Ruin, Desolate

Cease
(Verb)
Synonyms: End, Discontinue, Stop, Halt, Pause
Antonyms: Start, Continue, Begin, Carry on, Pursue

Celebrated
(Adjective)
Synonyms: Notable, Distinguished, Eminent, Noted, Illustrious
Antonyms: Unnoticed, Undistinguished, Unknown, Unnoted, Nameless

Celibacy
(Noun)
Synonyms: Single, Singleness, Bachelorhood, Virginity, Blessed, Maidenhood, Chastity
Antonyms: Engagement, Wedlock, Married state, Matrimony, Union, Nuptial tie

Censorship
(Noun)
Synonyms: Disapproval, Criticism, Blame
Antonyms: Approval, Commendation, Appreciation, Approbation

Central

(Adjective)

Synonyms: Inner, Interior, Mean, Median, Mid, Chief, Essential, Focal, Fundamental, Key, Primary, Principal

Antonyms: Exterior, Outer, Outermost, Minor, Secondary, Subordinate, Remote

Certain

(Adjective)

Synonyms: Positive, Definite, Indisputable, Sure, Actual, Unequivocal, Incontestable

Antonyms: Doubtful, Indefinite, Disputable, Uncertain, Ambiguous, Equivocal, Contestable

Change

(Verb)

Synonyms: Alter, Veer, Shift, Diversity, Modify, Convert, Transfigure, Transform, Transmute

Antonyms: Hold fast, Stand, Clinch, Fix, Maintain, Sustain, Stabilize, Give way

Chaos

(Adjective)

Synonyms: Disorder, Confusion, Jumble, Abysmal, Void

Antonyms: Organization, Government, Orderliness

Charity

(Noun)

Synonyms: Kindness, Benignity, Generosity, Philanthropy, Benevolence, Beneficence, Alms, Giving, Liberty

Antonyms: Meanness, Liberality, Greediness, Selfishness

Chase

(Verb)

Synonyms: Follow, Hunt, Pursue, Track, Run after, Course

Antonyms: Forgo, Renounce, Withdraw, Leave, Abandon, Forsake

Cheap
(Adjective)

Synonyms: Worthless, Inferior, Mean, Inexpensive, Common, Paltry
Antonyms: Worthy, Superior, Noble, Lofty, Honorable, Eminent, Expensive, Dear, Costly

Cheat
(Verb)

Synonyms: Deceive, Swindle, Dupe, Hoodwink, Defraud, Fleece, Gull, Hoax, Bilk, Delude
Antonyms: Fair, True, Aboveboard, Just

Check
(Verb)

Synonyms: Restrain, Stop, Impede, Hinder, Control, Curb, Subdue, Repress
Antonyms: Speed, Hurry, Expedite, Accelerate, Quicken, Hasten, Precipitate

Cheer
(Verb)

Synonyms: Animate, Comfort, Solace, Gladden, Enliven, Exhilarate, Applaud, Clap, Praise
Antonyms: Deject, Depress, Dishearten, Sadden, Discourage, Damp, Decry, Deprecate, Disparage, Vilify, Condemn, Condole

Cheerful
(Adjective)

Synonyms: Joyous, Blithe, Sunny, Happy, Bright, Gay, Lively
Antonyms: Sullen, Gloomy, Downcast, Miserable, Sad, Woebegone

Chief
(Adjective)

Synonyms: Premier, Main, Leading, Supreme, Cardinal, Principal

Antonyms: Petty, Lesser, Minor, Inconsiderable, Inferior, Subordinate, Junior, Subsidiary

Chief

(Noun)

Synonyms: Principal, Leader, Head, Caption, Chieftain, Ruler, Commander

Antonyms: Follower, Servant, Dependent, Parasite, Minion

Chill

(Adjective)

Synonyms: Coldness, Chilliness, Shivering, Bite, Frost

Antonyms: Warmth, Fire, Gleam, Glow, Bonfire, Fervor

Choice

(Noun)

Synonyms: Selection, Option, Alternative, Adoption, Preference

Antonyms: Refusal, Denial, Rejection, Cancellation

Choke

(Verb)

Synonyms: Strangle, Suffocate, Smother, Stifle, Throttle

Antonyms: Oxygenate, Freshen, Ventilate, Air

Choose

(Verb)

Synonyms: Select, Prefer, Pick, Elect, Cull

Antonyms: Reject, Discard, Renounce, Spurn, Disapprove

Circulate

(Verb)

Synonyms: Propagate, Spread, Advertise, Publish, Diffuse, Disseminate

Antonyms: Quieten, Silence, Hush, Repress

Claim

(Verb)

Synonyms: Right, Title, Maintain, Require, Assume, Challenge,

Demand
Antonyms: Waive, Drop, Forgo, Yield, Renounce

Class
(Verb)

Synonyms: Arrange, Group, Rank, Distribute, Dispose, Classify
Antonyms: Disarrange, Display, Upset, Disorder, Confuse, Derange

Clean
(Verb)

Synonyms: Purify, Clarify, Cleanse, Faultless, Immaculate, Spotless, Unblemished
Antonyms: Corrupt, Infect, Defile, Soil, Pollute, Taint

Clear
(Adjective)

Synonyms: Definite, District, Unmistakable, Explicit
Antonyms: Blurred, Confused, Doubtful, Foggy, Vague

Clever
(Adjective)

Synonyms: Talented, Gifted, Capable, Sharp, Dexterous, Smart, Natural
Antonyms: Foolish, Dull, Doltish, Incapable, Stupid

Cling
(Verb)

Synonyms: Clasp, Attach, Adhere, Stick, Cleave, Together, Hold, Embrace, Hug
Antonyms: Surrender, Give up, Forgo, Relinquish, Resign, Cede

Cloudy
(Adjective)

Synonyms: Dark, Dim, Gloomy, Murky, Foggy, Overcast
Antonyms: Sunny, Undimmed, Unclouded, Clear, Bright

Clutch
(Verb)
Synonyms: Grip, Seize, Catch, Grab, Grasp
Antonyms: Release, Liberate, Emancipate

Coarse
(Adjective)
Synonyms: Unpolished, Harsh, Indelicate, Unrefined, Rude, G r o s s
Antonyms: Polished, Polite, Elegant, Refined, Civilized, Genteel

Cold
(Adjective)
Synonyms: Wintry, Bleak, Chilled, Chilly, Cool, Frigid, Frosty, Gelid, Icy
Antonyms: Boiling, Tepid, Hot, Passionate, Warm, Balmy

Combat
(Noun)
Synonyms: War, Battle, Action, Contest, Conflict, Broil
Antonyms: Harmony, Peace, Concord, Amity, Agreement, Quite

Comfort
(Noun)
Synonyms: Ease, Rest, Leisure, Relaxation, Repose, Relief
Antonyms: Unrest, Discomfort, Restlessness, Agitation, Nervousness

Comfortable
(Adjective)
Synonyms: Pleasant, Agreeable, Pleasing, Delightful, Homely, Relaxing, Restful, Convenient, Cozy
Antonyms: Irritating, Disagreeable, Displeasing, Aggravating, Distressed, Disturbed

Command
(Noun)

Synonyms: Commandment, Order, Directive, Mandate, Rule, Behest, Decree, Direct
Antonyms: Comply, Submit, Obey, Beg, Beseech, Plead

Commemorate
(Verb)

Synonyms: Celebrate, Honor, Immortalize, Keep, Memorialize, Pay tribute to, Recógnize, Remember, Salute, Solemnize
Antonyms: Disregard, Forget, Ignore, Omit, Overlook, Pass over, Take no notice of

Common
(Adjective)

Synonyms: Usual, Frequent, Ordinary, Familiar, Vulgar, Mean, Hackneyed, Trite, Low
Antonyms: Unusual, Frequent, Extraordinary, Exceptional, Unfamiliar, Choice, Refined, Cultured, Polished, Gentle

Compact
(Adjective)

Synonyms: Compressed, Condensed, Dense, Firm, Impenetrable, Impermeable, Pressed together, Solid, Thick, Compendious, Concise, Epigrammatic, Laconic
Antonyms: Dispersed, Large, Loose, Roomy, Scattered, Spacious, Sprawling, Garrulous, Lengthy, Prolix, Rambling, Verbose, Wordy

Companion
(Noun)

Synonyms: Friend, Colleague, Pen-pal, Comrade, Shadow, Accomplice, Associate
Antonyms: Enemy, Rival, Partisan, Unsportsmanlike

Company
(Noun)

Synonyms: Collection, Crowd, Troupe, Assemblage, Group,

Gathering, Firm, Assembly, House, Gang, Conclave
Antonyms: Individual, Isolated, Alone, Single

Comparison
(Noun)
Synonyms: Similitude, Illustration, Simile, Collation, Juxtaposition, Correlation, Resemblance
Antonyms: Difference, Contrariety, Contrast, Contrary

Compassion
(Noun)
Synonyms: Kindness, Charity, Clemency, Sorrow, Tenderness, Mercy, Sympathy, Condolence
Antonyms: Cruelty, Malignity, Barbarity, Savagery

Compel
(Verb)
Synonyms: Bind, Coerce, Drive, Oblige, Constrain, Force, Necessitate
Antonyms: Acquit, Induce, Allure

Competent
(Adjective)
Synonyms: Skilful, Learned, Able, Adapted, Adequate, Appropriate, Capable, Clever, Endowed, Equal, Fit, Pertinent, Proficient, Qualified, Sufficient, Suitable
Antonyms: Inefficient, Inadequate, Incapable, Incompetent, Inexperienced, Inexpert, Unqualified, Unskilled

Complacent
(Adjective)
Synonyms: Content, Gratified, Pleased, Pleased with oneself, Resting on one's laurels, Satisfied self, Assured, Self-contented, Self satisfied, Serene, Smug, Unconcerned
Antonyms: Discontent, Dissatisfied, Insecure, Troubled, Uneasy, Unsatisfied

Compose
(Verb)

Synonyms: Write, Pacify, Form, Calm, Allay
Antonyms: Excite, Irritate, Criticize, Dissect

Compress
(Verb)

Synonyms: Abridge, Contract, Crowd, Compact, Condense
Antonyms: Diffuse, Dilate, Expand, Extend

Compromise
(Noun)

Synonyms: Compensation, Accommodation, Accord, Adjustment, Agreement, Concession, Half measures, Settlement
Antonyms: Hard-headedness, Contention, Controversy, Difference, Disagreement, Dispute, Quarrel

Compulsory
(Adjective)

Synonyms: Binding, Forced, Imperative, Mandatory, Obligatory, Required, Requisite
Antonyms: Discretionary, Elective, Optional, Unimperative, Unnecessary, Voluntary, Non-requisite

Conceal
(Verb)

Synonyms: Suppress, Screen, Disguise, Hide, Bury, Camouflage, Cover, Obscure, Secret
Antonyms: Expose, Confess, Avow, Manifest, Disclose, Divulge, Expose, Reveal

Concede
(Verb)

Synonyms: Admit, Accept, Acknowledge, Allow, Confess, Grant, Cede, Hand over, Relinquish, Surrender, Yield
Antonyms: Contest, Deny, Disclaim, Dispute, Protest, Refute, Reject, Boat, Conquer, Defeat

Conceited

(Adjective)

Synonyms: Arrogant, Egotistical, Immodest, Narcissistic, Overweening, Too big for one's boot, Vain

Antonyms: Humble, Modest, Self effecting, Unassuming

Concentration

(Noun)

Synonyms: Absorption, Application, Heed, Bringing, To bear, Centralization, Consolidation, Convergence, Accumulation, Aggregation, Collection, Horde

Antonyms: Absent-mindedness, Disregard, Distraction, Inattention, Diffusion, Disperse, Scattering, Spreading–out

Concerted

(Adjective)

Synonyms: Agreed upon, Collaborative, Combined, Coordinated, Joint, Planned, Prearranged, United

Antonyms: Disunited, Separate, Uncountrived, Uncooperative, Unplanned, Divided

Concord

(Noun)

Synonyms: Unity, Peace, Amity, Accord

Antonyms: Animosity, Variance, Discord, Disagreement

Concrete

(Adjective)

Synonyms: Consolidated, Compact, Firm

Antonyms: Loose, Shifting, Bogy, Sloppy

Confess

(Verb)

Synonyms: Acknowledge, Reveal, Own, Aver

Antonyms: Deny, Suppress, Disavow, Cover, Hide

Confine
(Verb)
Synonyms: Bind, Narrow, Bound, Limit, Immune, Impute
Antonyms: Extend, Expand, Loosen, Widen, Dilate

Confirm
(Verb)
Synonyms: Countersign, Verify, Fix, Prove, Strengthen, Settle
Antonyms: Countermand, Invalidate, Cancel, Upset, Refute, Repeal, Shake

Conquest
(Noun)
Synonyms: Overthrow, Victory, Triumph
Antonyms: Forfeiture, Surrender, Retreat, Defeat

Conscientious
(Adjective)
Synonyms: Principled, Careful, Diligent, Faithful, Uncorrupt, Meticulous, Responsible
Antonyms: Careless, Corrupt, Negligent, Slack, Profligate, Wicked, Vile

Considerable
(Adjective)
Synonyms: Thoughtful, Attentive, Heedful, Circumspect, Kind
Antonyms: Thoughtless, Inattentive, Heedless, Negligent, Unconcerned

Considerate
(Adjective)
Synonyms: Attentive, Careful, Reflective, Unselfish, Tactful, Helpful, Thoughtful
Antonyms: Rude, Heedless, Negligent

Constant
(Adjective)
Synonyms: Steady, Firm, Unswerving, Ceaseless, Everlasting, Incessant, Steadfast

Antonyms: Unsteady, Flexible, Variable, Inconsonant, Unreliable, Unstable, Fickle

Contemptible

(Adjective)

Synonyms: Despicable, Paltry, Pitiful, Vile, Detestable, Execrable

Antonyms: Respectable, Admirable, Excellent, Weighty, Grave, Important

Consumption

(Noun)

Synonyms: Extinction, Decline, Waste, Expenditure, Dissipation, Destruction

Antonyms: Preservation, Increase, Gain, Income, Accumulation, Addition

Contented

(Adjective)

Synonyms: Satisfied, Gratified, Pleased, Cheerful, Comfortable, Serene, Happy

Antonyms: Discontent, Frustrated, Malcontent, Miserable

Contract

(Noun)

Synonyms: Agreement, Arrangement, Bargain, Bond, Commitment, Compact, Convention, Covenant, Engagement, Settlement treaty

Antonyms: Decline, Disagree, Refuse, Enlarge, Expend, Grow, Increase, Multiply, Spread, Stretch, Swell

Controversy

(Noun)

Synonyms: Unbind, Dispute, Argument, Contention, Bickering, Debate

Antonyms: Agreement, Compromise, Accord, Unanimity

Convenient
(Adjective)

Synonyms: Suitable, Comfortable, Adapted, Handy, Advantageous
Antonyms: Untoward, Inconvenient, Cumbersome, Heavy

Conventional
(Adjective)

Synonyms: Accepted, Formal, Habitual, Normal, Correct, Common, Orthodox, Prevailing, Prevalent, Traditional, Usual, Stereotyped, Hackneyed
Antonyms: Uncommon, Unusual, Off-the-wall, Left–field, Unconventional, Unorthodox

Convict
(Verb)

Synonyms: Condemn, Sentence, Imprison, Culprit
Antonyms: Discharge, Acquit, Innocent

Cooperate
(Verb)

Synonyms: Work together, Abet, Concur, Aid, Assist, Contribute
Antonyms: Conflict, Opposed, Rival, Thwarting, Fight, Hamper, Hinder, Obstruct, Prevent

Cordial
(Adjective)

Synonyms: Hearty, Sincere, Warm, Earnest
Antonyms: Formal, Distant, Ceremonious, Cold

Correspond
(Verb)

Synonyms: Accord, Agree, Coincide, Complement, Conform, Correlate, Dovetail, Fit, Harmonize, Match, Square
Antonyms: Be at variance, Be dissimilar, Be inconsistent, Belie, Unlike, Differ, Disagree, Diverge

Corrupt
(Verb)
Synonyms: Pollute, Impair, Spoil, Putrefy, Defile, Infected, Decayed, Violated, Defiled
Antonyms: Cleanse, Purify, Repair, Mend, Pure, Undefiled, Uncorrupt, Uninfected

Cover
(Verb)
Synonyms: Hide, Screen, Shield, Veil, Project, Mask
Antonyms: Expose, Unveil, Uncover, Exhibit

Courage
(Noun)
Synonyms: Bravery, Boldness, Heroism, Intrepidity, Valor, Mettle
Antonyms: Cowardice, Timidity, Diffidence, Pusillanimity

Creed
(Noun)
Synonyms: Belief, Faith, Confession, Catechism, Dogma, Doctrine, Tenet
Antonyms: Disbelief, Recantation, Protest, Abjuration

Crime
(Noun)
Synonyms: Sin, Evil, Wrong-doing, Offence, Outrange, Guilt, Felony
Antonyms: Modesty, Incorruption, Guiltlessness, Blamelessness, Artlessness

Cripple
(Verb)
Synonyms: Disable, Curtail, Cramp, Impair, Weaken
Antonyms: Free, Ease, Renovate, Augment

Cruel

(Adjective)

Synonyms: Unfeeling, Inhuman, Merciless, Inexorable, Callous, Pitiless

Antonyms: Human, Merciful, Sympathetic, Tender, Kind, Compassionate

Cunning

(Adjective)

Synonyms: Crafty, Artful, Astute, Devious, Guileful, Machiavellian, Skilful, Adroit, Shrewd, Sly, Subtle

Antonyms: Artless, Dull, Ethical, Frank, Honest, Ingenious, Maladroit

Curious

(Adjective)

Synonyms: Inquiring, Inquisitive, Interested, Puzzled, Searching, Inquisitive, Meddling, Peeping, Pressing, Unusual, Extraordinary, Mysterious, Peculiar

Antonyms: Incurious, Indifferent, Uninterested, Common, Everyday, Familiar, Ordinary

Customary

(Adjective)

Synonyms: Usual, Accepted, Accustomed, Common, Confirmed, Conventional, Established, Everyday, Familiar, Fashionable, General, Habitual, Normal, Ordinary, Popular, Regular, Routine, Traditional, Wanted

Antonyms: Exceptional, Infrequent, Irregular, Occasional, Rare, Uncommon, Unusual

Current

(Adjective)

Synonyms: Popular, Present, Ordinary, Prevalent

Antonyms: Rejected, Private, Confined, Secret

Cynical

(Adjective)

Synonyms: Skeptical, Contemptuous, Derisive, Distrustful, Ironic, Misanthropic, Mocking, Mordacious, Pessimistic, Sarcastic, Sardonic, Scoffing, Scornful, Sneering, Unbelieving

Antonyms: Credulous, Green, Gullible, Hopeful, Optimistic, Trustful, Trusting, Unsceptical, Unsuspecting

D

Dainty

(Adjective)

Synonyms: Delicate, Charming, Elegant, Exquisite, Fine, Graceful, Neat, Petite, Pretty, Choice, Delicious, Palatable, Savoury, Choosy, Fastidious, Finial fancy, Sweetmeat, Tidbit

Antonyms: Awkward, Clumsy, Coarse, Gauche, Inelegant, Maladroit, Uncouth, Ungainly

Dally

(Verb)

Synonyms: Dawdle, Delay, Drag one's feet or heel, Linger, Loiter, Procrastinate, Tarry, Caress, Fondle, Tamper, Tease, Toy, Trifle

Antonyms: Hasten, Hurry up, Make haste, Push, Forward or on, Run, Step on it

Danger

(Noun)

Synonyms: Insecurity, Risk, Peril, Hazard, Menace, Threat, Jeopardy

Antonyms: Protection, Safeguard, Defense, Safety, Security

Dark

(Adjective)

Synonyms: Cloudy, Dim, Dingy, Murky, Overcast, Pitchy, Shadowy, Dusky, Sable, Bleak, Dismal, Morbid, Morose, Sad, Somber, Abstruse, Arcane

Antonyms: Blond, Blonde, Fair, Fair-haired, Flaxen-Haired, Light, Bright, Cheerful, Clear, Genial, Glad, Hopeful, Pleasant

Dazzling
(Adjective)

Synonyms: Brilliant, Divine, Glittering, Glorious, Radiant, Scintillating, Shining, Sparkling, Stunning, Sublime, Superb, Virtuoso

Antonyms: Dull, Ordinary, Tedious, Unexceptional, Unexciting, Uninspiring, Uninteresting, Unmemorable, Unremarkable

Damn
(Verb)

Synonyms: Blast, Castigate, Censure, Condemn, Denounce, Denunciate, Excoriate, Inveigh, Abuse, Blaspheme, Execrate, Imprecate, Revile, Sentence

Antonyms: Acclaim, Admire, Applaud, Approve, Cheer, Compliment, Congratulate, Extol, Honor, Laud, Praise, Adore, Bless, Exalt, Glorify, Pay homage to

Damp
(Adjective)

Synonyms: Clammy, Dark, Dewy, Dripping, Drizzly, Humid, Misty, Muggy, Sodden, Sopping, Vaporous, Wet, Allay, Check, Chill, Cool, Dash, Deaden, Dull, Reduce

Antonyms: Arid, Dry, Watertight, Encouraging, Gee, Up, Hearten, Inspire

Deadly
(Adjective)

Synonyms: Fatal, Baleful, Mortal, Noxious, Pernicious, Poisonous, Venomous

Antonyms: Vital, Healthful, Life-giving, Nutritious

Decay
(Noun)

Synonyms: Fail, Deterioration, Sinking, Decline, Wearing, Degeneracy

Antonyms: Improvement, Progress, Expansion, Development, Growth

Deceive
(Verb)

Synonyms: Betray, Dupe, Entrap, Cheat, Trick
Antonyms: Enlighten, Guide, Deliver, Advise

Deception
(Noun)

Synonyms: Fraud, Deceit, Trickery, Chicanery, Equivocation
Antonyms: Sincerity, Veracity, Honesty, Candor, Frankness

Decide
(Verb)

Synonyms: Settle, Fixed, Determine, Choose, Conclude, Decree, Elect, Resolve
Antonyms: Hesitate, Doubt, Fluctuation, Vacillate, Be indecisive

Declare
(Verb)

Synonyms: Announce, Broadcast, Publish, Proclaim, Advertise, Enunciate
Antonyms: Conceal, Censor, Withhold, Deny

Decline
(Verb)

Synonyms: Reject, Refuse, Discard, Renounce, Sink, Degenerate, Decrease, Lessen, Fall, Drop
Antonyms: Accept, Accede to, Agree to, Admit, Grow, Aggravate, Enhance, Increase

Decrease
(Verb)

Synonyms: Reduce, Decline, Subside, Diminish, Lessen
Antonyms: Increase, Enlarge, Enhance, Extend, Argument, Advance, Intensify

Deed
(Noun)
Synonyms: Victory, Action, Feat, Exploit, Work, Achievement
Antonyms: Inertness, Restful, Unemployment, Passivity, Dullness, Fatigue, Dawdling, Dormancy, Delay

Defeat
(Verb)
Synonyms: Overcome, Rout, Outwit, Frustration, Foil
Antonyms: Prevail, Triumph, Win, Overthrow, Vanquish

Definite
(Adjective)
Synonyms: Exact, Certain, Specific, Fixed, Definite, Explicit, Express, Unconditional, Unqualified, Categorical, Unequivocal
Antonyms: Indefinite, Unspecified, Unspecific, Vague, Obscure, Tentative, Ambiguous, Implicit, Uncertain, Conditional

Delay
(Verb)
Synonyms: Hold, Keep, Detain, Retard
Antonyms: Quicken, Speed, Send, Accelerate, Advance, Expedite, Rush, Hasten, Hurry, Further

Delicacy
(Noun)
Synonyms: Smoothness, Softness, Nicety, Elegance, Refinement, Slenderness, Lightness,
Antonyms: Roughness, Hardness, Robustness, Crudeness, Heaviness

Deliver
(Verb)
Synonyms: Consign, Cede, Free, Discharge, Liberate, Surrender, Release, Rescue, Save, Yield, Relinquish, Handover
Antonyms: Arrest, Imprison, Capture, Apprehend, Catch, Seize, Adopt, Withhold, Keep, Appropriate

Denigrate

(Verb)

Synonyms: Asperse, Belittle, Besmirch, Blacken, Calumniate, Decry, Defame, Disparage, Impugn, Malign, Revile, Slander, Vilify

Antonyms: Acclaim, Admire, Approve, Cheer, Compliment, Eulogize, Extol, Honor, Laud, Praise, Take one's hat off to

Deny

(Verb)

Synonyms: Contradict, Disagree with, Disprove, Oppose, Rebuff, Rebut, Refute, Refuse, Begrudge, Decline, Disallow, Forbid, Reject, Veto, Abjure

Antonyms: Accept, Acknowledge, Admit, Affirm, Agree, Allow, Concede, Confirm, Recognize, Grant, Let, Permit, Receive

Dependence

(Noun)

Synonyms: Slavery, Helplessness, Thraldom, Reliance

Antonyms: Delivery, Permission, License, Independence, Discharge, Play, Latitude, Release, Free, Trade, Swing, Fullscap

Depraved

(Adjective)

Synonyms: Abandoned, Corrupt, Debased, Debauched, Degenerate, Degraded, Dissolute, Evil, Immoral, Lascivious, Lewd, Licentious, Perverted, Profligate, Shameless, Sinful, Vicious, Vile, Wicked

Antonyms: Chaste, Decent, Ethical, Good, Honorable, Innocent, Moral, Proper, Pure, Upright, Virtuous, Wholesome

Depreciate

(Verb)

Synonyms: Decrease, Deflate, Devaluate, Lessen, Lower, Reduce, Disparage, Denigrate, Deride, Detract, Ridicule, Scorn, Traduce, Underestimate

Antonyms: Add to, Appreciate, Augment, Enhance, Enlarge,

Expand, Grow, Increase, Use, Admire, Cherish, Esteem, Like, Prize, Regard, Respect, Value

Describe
(Verb)

Synonyms: Explain, Relate, Illustrate, Tell, Draw, Define, Narrate, Recount, Picture
Antonyms: Falsify, Mystify, Misrepresent, Suppress, Obscure, Misinterpret

Despair
(Noun)

Synonyms: Despondency, Dejection, Desperation, Hopelessness, Discouragement
Antonyms: Confidence, Encouragement, Elation, Hopefulness, Expectation, Hope, Optimism

Despise
(Verb)

Synonyms: Hate, Abhor, Scorn, Loathe, Disdain
Antonyms: Admire, Adore, Like, Love, Respect, Appreciate

Destroy
(Verb)

Synonyms: Wither, Ravage, Kill, Ruin, Raze, Uproot, Wreck, Waste, Demolish, Annihilate, Eradicate, Exterminate, Extinguish
Antonyms: Rootage, Rooted, Make, Repair, Restore, Reinstate, Build, Create, Devise, Establish

Destruction
(Noun)

Synonyms: Devastation, Demolition, Desolation, Annihilation, Subversion
Antonyms: Creation, Production, Making, Construction

Detrimental
(Adjective)

Synonyms: Adverse, Baleful, Damaging, Deleterious,

Destructive, Disadvantages, Harmful, Inimical, Injurious, Mischievous, Pernicious, Prejudicial, Unfavorable
Antonyms: Advantageous, Beneficial, Efficacious, Favorable, Good, Helpful, Salutary

Develop
(Verb)

Synonyms: Expand, Clear, Unfold, Disclose, lay, Open
Antonyms: Obscure, Conceal, Wrap, Envelop

Deviate
(Verb)

Synonyms: Change, Diverge, Swerve, Stray, Ramble, Wander, Err, Vary, Differ
Antonyms: Coverage, Stay, Perpetuate, Continue, Pervade, Abide

Devoted
(Adjective)

Synonyms: Loving, Affectionate, Assiduous, Dedicated, Fond, Ardent
Antonyms: Unfaithful, Faithless, Indifferent, Cool, Disloyal

Diligent
(Adjective)

Synonyms: Careful, Laborious, Attentive, Busy, Painstaking
Antonyms: Slack, Lazy, Indolent, Idle, Slothful

Dim
(Adjective)

Synonyms: Cloudy , Dark, Darkish, Dusky, Overcast, Tenebrous, Bleary, Blurred, Faint, Obscured, Dense, Dull, Obtuse, Unclear, Stupid
Antonyms: Bright, Clear, Cloudless, Fair, Pleasant, Sunny, Brilliant, Limpid, Acute, Astute, Clever, Intelligent, Keen, Sharp, Smart

Diplomatic
(Adjective)
Synonyms: Discreet, Prudent, Shrewd, Sagacious, Judicious, Sharp, Astute
Antonyms: Indiscreet, Imprudent, Tackles, Injudicious, Silly, Bungling

Dirty
(Adjective)
Synonyms: Foul, Filthy, Squalid, Soiled, Unclean, Sordid, Impure
Antonyms: Clean, Pure, Unsoiled, Unsullied, Virginal

Disappoint
(Verb)
Synonyms: Defeat, Vex, Baffle, Foil, Deceive, Betray
Antonyms: Satisfy, Gratify, Fulfill, Justify

Disclose
(Verb)
Synonyms: Reveal, Uncover, Confess, Expose, Unveil, Betray, Unfold
Antonyms: Conceal, Cover, Suppress, Hide, Veil, Dissemble, Cloak

Disgrace
(Noun)
Synonyms: Dishonor, Shame, Degrade, Discredit, Disparage, Humiliate, Desert
Antonyms: Honor, Reverence, Respect, Exalt, Dignify, Elevate, Venerate

Displace
(Verb)
Synonyms: Dislocate, Remove, Oust, Supplant, Supersede
Antonyms: Establish, Settle, Set, Secure, Root, Plant

Dissolve
(Verb)
Synonyms: Divide, Disunite, Separate, Break up, Disperse, Part , Disconnect
Antonyms: Unite, Combine, Concert, Join, Conjoin, Amalgamate, Connect

Distant
(Adjective)
Synonyms: Faraway, Inaccessible, Remote, Asunder
Antonyms: Accessible, Close, Proximate, Contiguous, Adjacent

Diversity
(Noun)
Synonyms: Variegate, Modify, Alter, Vary
Antonyms: Solidify, Unity, Fix, Conserve

Dogged
(Adjective)
Synonyms: Determined, Firm, Immovable, Indefatigable, Obstinate, Persevering, Persistent, Pertinacious, Resolute, Steadfast, Stubborn
Antonyms: Doubtful, Halfhearted, Hesitant, Irresolute, Undetermined, Unsteady

Doubt
(Noun)
Synonyms: Suspicion, Skepticism, Uncertainty, Dubiety
Antonyms: Certainty, Confidence, Conviction, Assurance

Doubtful
(Adjective)
Synonyms: Uncertain, Dubious, Questionable, Problematic, Equivocal, Ambiguous
Antonyms: Clear, Confident, Definite, Decided, Sure, Certain

Dreadful
(Adjective)
Synonyms: Fearful, Frightful, Dire, Afraid, Alarming, Horrible,

Awful, Terrific
Antonyms: Pleasing, Pleasurable, Propitious, Reassuring, Auspicious

Dry
(Adjective)
Synonyms: Parched, Arid, Barren, Tedious, Dehydrated, Crisp, Desiccated
Antonyms: Damp, Wet, Moistened, Fresh, Lively, Moist, Soggy

Dull
(Adjective)
Synonyms: Tiresome, Monotonous, Uninteresting, Irksome, Boring, Dreary
Antonyms: Interesting, Spirited, Enthralling, Lively

E

Eager

(Adjective)

Synonyms: Desirous, Anxious, Fervent, Impatient, Zealous, Enthusiastic, Keen

Antonyms: Cool, Unconcerned, Indifferently, Apathetic, Loath, Disinterested

Earn

(Verb)

Synonyms: Obtain, Gain, Win, Achieve, Acquire, Merit

Antonyms: Alienate, Lose, Waste, Spend, Forgo, Forfeit

Easy

(Adjective)

Synonyms: A bed of roses, Child's play, Clear, Effortless, Facile, Light, Simple, Carefree, Calm, Comfortable, Contented, Peaceful, Serene, Tranquil, Tolerant, Lenient, Mild, Affable, Easygoing

Antonyms: Arduous, Complex, Difficult, Formidable, Onerous, Stressful, Hard, Harsh, Rigid, Stern, Anxious, Formal, Unnatural, Impossible

Ebb

(Verb)

Synonyms: Wane, Decline, Decay, Sink, Recede, Retire

Antonyms: Flow, Increase, Abound, Swell

Elegant

(Adjective)

Synonyms: Elaborate, Luxurious, Grandiose, Sumptuous,

Deluxe
Antonyms: Inexpensive, Plain, Mediocre, Unadorned, Simple and vulgar

Emit
(Verb)

Synonyms: Breathe forth, Cast out, Diffuse, Discharge, Eject, Emanate, Exhale, Exude, Give out, Give, Vent to, Issue, Radiate, Send forth, Send out, Throw out, Transmit
Antonyms: Absorb, Assimilate, Consume, Devour, Digest, Drink in, Incorporate, Ingest, Receive, Soak up, Such up, Take in

Emotion
(Noun)

Synonyms: Agitation, Tremor, Passion, Feeling, Sentiment, Desire
Antonyms: Stoicism, Insensibility, Rationality, Reason, Indifferences

Enchanted
(Adjective)

Synonyms: Fascinated, Bewitched, Captivated, Enraptured, Enamored, Entranced, Spellbound, Charmed
Antonyms: Disgusted, Repulsed, Replied, Nauseated

Encourage
(Verb)

Synonyms: Back up, Animate, Urge, Reassure, Incite, Cheer, Embolden, Foster, Hearten, Support, Promote
Antonyms: Dissuade, Discourage, Abash, Dishearten, Thwart, Hinder

Encroach
(Verb)

Synonyms: Infringe, Violate, Invade, Intrude, Trespass
Antonyms: Desist, Observe, Respect, Withdraw

Endanger

(Verb)

Synonyms: Venture, Hazard, Jeopardize, Risk, Imperil
Antonyms: Protect, Safeguard, Shield, Defend, Screen

Endless

(Adjective)

Synonyms: Unlimited, Limitless, Interminable, Unceasing, Boundless, Eternal, Infinite
Antonyms: Discontinuous, Finite, Short, Temporary, Brief, Fugitive, Limited

Endorse

(Verb)

Synonyms: Approve, Accredit, Ratify, Confirm, Sanction
Antonyms: Discredit, Condemn, Censure, Disapprove, Reject, Reprehend

Enduring

(Adjective)

Synonyms: Abiding, Continuing, Durable, Firm, Immortal, Immovable, Imperishable, Fasting, Living, Perennial, Permanent, Persistent, Prevailing, Remaining, Surviving
Antonyms: Brief, Ephemeral, Fleeting, Momentary, Passing, Short, Short-lived, Temporary, Transient, Transitory

Enlarge

(Verb)

Synonyms: Augment, Expand, Amplify, Magnify, Increase
Antonyms: Contract, Condense, Narrow, Shorten, Reduce, Decrease

Enmity

(Noun)

Synonyms: Hostility, Hate, Discord, Animus, Rancor, Animosity, Antagonism
Antonyms: Amity, Love, Harmony, Fellowship, Sympathy

Enormous
(Adjective)

Synonyms: Astronomic, Colossal , Elephantine, Excessive, Gargantuan, Gigantic, Gross, Immense, Mammoth, Massive, Monstrous, Mountainous, Prodigious, Titanic, Tremendous, Vast

Antonyms: Diminutive, Dwarf, Infinitesimal, Insignificant, Lilliputain, Little, Meager, Microscopic, Meager, Minute, Petite, Small, Tiny, Trivial, Wee

Enough
(Adjective)

Synonyms: Sufficient , Adequate, Plenty, Abundant, Ample

Antonyms: Insufficient, Inadequate, Scarcity, Deficient

Enrage
(Verb)

Synonyms: Anger, Madden, Incense, Infuriate

Antonyms: Pacify, Mollify, Soothe, Tranquilize, Placate

Entire
(Adjective)

Synonyms: Undivided, Unbroken, Whole, Full, Complete, Intact, Total

Antonyms: Broken, Partial, Divided, Damaged, Destroyed, Empty, Imperfect, Incomplete, Limited

Erase
(Verb)

Synonyms: Abolish, Destroy, Efface, Eradicate, Obliterate, Cancel, Delete

Antonyms: Impress, Imprint, Insert, Confirm, Establish, Reinstate

Eternal
(Adjective)

Synonyms: Perpetual, Ceaseless, Deathless, Unending

Antonyms: Temporal, Fleeting, Swift, Passing

Evasion
(Noun)
Synonyms: Tergiversation, Quibble, Subterfuge, Prevarication, Excuse, Pretext
Antonyms: Refutation, Reply, Rejoinder, Response, Defence, Answer

Evident
(Adjective)
Synonyms: Clear, Visible, Obvious, Evident, Patent, Manifest, Distinct
Antonyms: Hidden, Obscure, Secret, Covert, Latent, Masked

Exact
(Adjective)
Synonyms: Unerring, Truthful, Correct, Careful, Precise, Strict
Antonyms: Inexact, Erring, Incorrect, Careless, Negligent, Untruthful

Excellent
(Adjective)
Synonyms: Select, First - class, Prime, First - rate, Choice
Antonyms: Mediocre, Faulty, Imperfect, Poor, Second–class

Excite
(Verb)
Synonyms : Stimulate, Provoke, Arise, Awake, Inflame, Animate, Kindle, Irritate
Antonyms: Compose, Soothe, Allay, Hush, Mollify, Quell, Appease, Quieten, Pacify, Lull

Exertion
(Noun)
Synonyms: Energy, Strain, Effort, Stretch, Pull, Tug, Spurt, Struggle, Pain, Trouble, Endeavour
Antonyms: Rest, Repose, Peace, Tranquility, Idleness, Laziness, Lethargy

Extend

(Verb)

Synonyms: Expand, Increase, Augment, Grow, Lengthen, Protract, Wide, Stretch, Elongate, Prolong

Antonyms: Reduce, Decrease, Curtail, Contract, Shorten, Narrow, Shrink, Terminate, Truncate

Extravagant

(Adjective)

Synonyms : Unreasonable, Excessive, Immoderate, Inordinate, Spendthrift, Lavish, Profuse, Wasteful, Prodigal

Antonyms: Reasonable, Judicious, Moderate, Temperate, Economical, Provident, Thrifty, Sparing

F

Fabulous

(Adjective)

Synonyms: Brilliant, Fantastic, Marvelous, Spectacular, Superb, Amazing, Breathtaking, Fictitious, Immense, Incredible, Wonderful, Astounding

Antonyms: Actual, Common, Commonplace, Credible, Genuine, Natural, Ordinary, Real

Face

(Noun)

Synonyms: Physignomy, Visage, Surface, Appearance, Front, Expression

Antonyms: Back, Invisible, Concealment

Facility

(Noun).

Synonyms: Easiness, Smoothness, Smooth, Pilancy, Flexibility, Capability, Dexterity, Skill, Waver

Antonyms: Difficulty, Hardness, Uphill, Tough job, Hard task, crossfire, Net, Puzzle

Fact

(Noun)

Synonyms: Certainty, Event, Reality, Phenomenon

Antonyms: Falsehood, Untruth, Lying, Forgery, Fraud, Fencing, Shuffling, Deceit

Failure

(Noun)

Synonyms: Breakdown, Collapse, Default, Neglect, Insolvency, Bankruptcy, Ruin, Neglect

Antonyms: Attainment, Achievement, Victory, Success, Triumph

Faithfulness

(Noun)

Synonyms: Loyalty, Constancy, Steadfastness, Fidelity, Devotion

Antonyms: Disloyalty, Inconstancy, Untrustworthiness, Unfaithfulness, Infidelity

False

(Adjective)

Synonyms: Untrue, Unreliable, Fallacious, Untruthful, Fictitious, Incorrect, Bogus, Misleading, Deceptive

Antonyms: True, Truthful, Authentic, Correct

Fame

(Noun)

Synonyms: Reputation, Honor, Glory, Renown, Esteem, Celebrity, Credit, Repute, Reputation

Antonyms: Disrepute, Dishonor, Notoriety, Oblivion

Famous

(Adjective)

Synonyms: Noted, Celebrated, Renowned, Well-Known

Antonyms: Obscure, Fugitive, Inglorious, Unknown

Fanciful

(Adjective)

Synonyms: Imaginary, Unreal, Imaginative, Fantastic, Capricious, Whimsical

Antonyms: Positive, Realistic, Existent, Substantial, Factual, Veritable

Fasten
(Verb)
Synonyms: Join, Bind, Fix, Anchor, Bolt, Grip, Connect
Antonyms: Loose, Undo, Unfix

Fat
(Adjective)
Synonyms: Stout, Portly, Obese, Plump, Adipose, Chubby, Buxom
Antonyms : Emaciated, Thin, Slim

Fatal
(Adjective)
Synonyms: Lethal, Mortal, Deadly, Destructive, Pernicious, Baneful
Antonyms: Life- giving, Helpful, Beneficial, Constructive

Fear
(Noun)
Synonyms: Awe, Apprehension, Fright, Horror, Alarm, Panic, Terror, Dread
Antonyms: Pluck, Bravery, Trust, Courage, Calmness, Equanimity

Feeble
(Adjective)
Synonyms: Weak, Impotent, Frail, Languid, Debilitated, Infirm
Antonyms: Strong, Vigorous, Muscular, Athletic, Stalwart, Robust, Sinewy

Filthy
(Adjective)
Synonyms: Dirty, Squalid, Foul, Impure, Sullied, Unclear
Antonyms: Pure, Clean, Immaculate, Spotless, Unsullied, Unsoiled

Final

(Adjective)

Synonyms: Last, Ultimate, Concluding, Finishing
Antonyms: First, Beginning, Opening, Initial

Find

(Verb)

Synonyms: Locate, Learn, Unearth, Detect, Ascertain, Discover
Antonyms: Forget, Miss, Mislay, Misplace, Overlook

Finish

(Verb)

Synonyms: Close, Shape, End, Conclude, Complete, Perfect, Finalize
Antonyms: Begin, Start, Open, Initiate

Foresight

(Noun)

Synonyms: Foreknowledge, Care, Caution, Precaution, Prudence, Forethought, Prescience, Presentiment, Foreshadowing
Antonyms: Narrow, mindedness, Bias, Shortsightedness, Prejudice

Fright

(Noun)

Synonyms: Apprehension, Alarm, Horror, Dismay, Panic, Terror, Trepidation, Fear, Dismay, Dread
Antonyms: Tranquility, Calmness, Coolness, Equanimity, Placidity, Composure

Fraud

(Noun)

Synonyms: Deceit, Duplicity, Stratagem, Chicanery, Guile, Hoax, Fake, Scam, Swindling, Deception
Antonyms: Honesty, Probity, Integrity, Fairness, Rectitude, Trustworthiness

Former

(Adjective)

Synonyms: Antecedent, Anterior, Earlier, Erstwhile, Prior, Quondam, Ancient, Departed, Old, Previous-part, Aforementioned, Aforesaid

Antonyms : Coming, Current, Ensuring, Following, Future, Latter, Subsequent, Succeeding, Modern, Present, Present day

Futile

(Adjective)

Synonyms: Abortive, Barren, Bootless, Empty, Forlorn, Fruitless, Hollow, In vain, Ineffectual, Profitless, Unproductive Unsuccessful, Worthless, Useless, Trivial, Idle, Trifling, Unimportant

Antonyms: Constructive, Effective, Fruitful, Profitable, Purposeful, Successful, Useful, Variable, Worthwhile, Important, Significant

Fundamental

(Adjective)

Synonyms : Essential, Important, Primary, Basic, Crucial, First, Integral

Antonyms : Secondary, Unimportant, Nonessential, Extra subsidiary, Superfluous

G

Gallant

(Adjective)

Synonyms: Bold, Brave, Courageous, Daring, Dashing, Heroic, Lion - hearted, Valiant, Valorous, August, Dignified, Glorious, Magnificent, Splendid

Antonyms: Cowardly, Fearful, Ignoble, Churlish, Discourteous, Ill-mannered, Impolite, Rude

Gather

(Verb)

Synonyms: Congregate, Collect, Muster, Convene, Accumulate, Amass, Flock, Group, Heap, Marshal, Assemble,

Antonyms: Disband, Scatter, Separate, Diffuse, Disperse, Dissipate

Gay

(Adjective)

Synonyms: Cheerful, Jovial, Vivacious, Jolly, Sprightly, Buoyant, Joyous, Blithe

Antonyms: Mournful, Cheerless, Unhappy, Depressed, Gloomy, Sorrowful, Sad, Dismal

General

(Adjective)

Synonyms: Common, Usual, Ordinary, Indefinite, Popular, Public, Universal, Accepted

Antonyms: Exceptional, Rare, Uncommon, Unusual, Queer, Specific

Generous
(Adjective)

Synonyms: Liberal, Noble, Lavish, Bountiful, Magnanimous
Antonyms: Greed, Niggardly, Chary, Sparing, Light, Selfish, Parsimonious

Genial
(Adjective)

Synonyms: Affable, Agreeable, Amiable, Cheerful, Cheery, Congenial, Convivial, Cordial, Easy - going, Enlivening, Friendly, Glad, Happy, Hearty, Jolly, Merry, Pleasant, Sunny, Warm
Antonyms: Cheerless, Coo, Discourteous, Frigid, Morose, Rude, Sardonic, Sullen, Unfriendly, Ungracious, Unpleasant

Genuine
(Adjective)

Synonyms: Authentic, Pure, Real, Actual, True, Sincere
Antonyms : Fictitious, Spurious, Artificial, Fake, Forged, Imaginary

Glorify
(Verb)

Synonym: Extol, Adore, Canonize , Enshrine, Revere, Venerate, Exalt, Commend, Appraise
Antonyms: Abuse, Depress, Reject, Debase, Defile, Degrade, Humiliate, Mock, Condemn

Gifted
(Adjective)

Synonyms : Intelligent, Able, Apt, Skillful, Sagacious, Talented, Adroit, Expert, Clever, Ingenious
Antonyms: Foolish, Stupid, Idiotic, Stolid, Amateur, Dull, Inept, Remanded

Gorgeous
(Adjective)

Synonyms: Sumptuous, Magnificent, Splendid, Grand,

Beautiful, Brilliant, Dazzling, Elegant
Antonyms: Colorless, Simple, Unadorned, Somber, Ugly, Cheap, Shabby, Shoddy

Gradual
(Adjective)
Synonyms: Slow, Steady, Moderate, Piecemeal, Gentle, Regular, Continuous, Progressive
Antonyms: Rapid, Momentary, Unanticipated, Unpremeditated, Unforeseen

Grand
(Adjective)
Synonyms: Superb, Noble, Majestic, Lordly, Stately, Resplendent, August, Exalted, Illustrious
Antonyms: Inferior, Colorless, Ignoble, Undignified, Awful, Mean, Worthless

Grasp
(Verb)
Synonyms: Hold, Seize, Snatch, Grip, Grab, Clutch, Clasp
Antonyms: Loose, Lose, Abandon, Release, Relinquish

Grief
(Noun)
Synonyms: Pain, Sorrow, Trouble, Grievance, Remorse, Suffering, Tribulation, Trouble, Woe, Affection, Bereavement, Distress
Antonyms: Glee, Joy, Contentment, Satisfaction, Rejoicing, Solace, Happiness, Pleasure

Grim
(Adjective)
Synonyms: Cruel, Ferocious, Fierce, Formidable, Frightful, Ghastly, Grisly, Gruesome, Hard, Harsh, Horrible, Merciless, Ruthless, Severe, Sullen, Surly, Terrible
Antonyms: Amiable, Attractive, Benign, Cheerful, Easy, Genial, Gentle, Happy, Kind, Pleasant, Soft, Sympathetic

Groundless

(Adjective)

Synonyms: False, Baseless, Unauthorized, Gratuitous, Fanciful

Antonyms: Actual, Material, Well-founded, Substantial, Positive, Real, Solid

H

Habitual

(Adjective)

Synonyms: Accustomed, Common, Familiar, Fixed, Natural, Ordinary, Standard, Customary, Chronic, Constant, Established, Frequent, Inveterate, Recurrent, Persistent

Antonyms: Abnormal, Exceptional, Extraordinary, Rare, Strange, Uncommon, Unusual, Infrequent, Irregular, Occasional

Halt

(Verb)

Synonyms: Break off, Cease, Close down, Come to an end, Desist, Draw up, Stand, Wait, Check, Curb, Nip in the bud, Terminate, Obstruct

Antonyms: Begin, Commence, Continue, Go ahead, Maintain, Proceed, Resume, Start, Aid, Boost, Encourage, Forward

Hamper

(Verb)

Synonyms : Bind, Cramp, Curb, Encumber, Entangle, Fetter, Frustrate, Hamstring, Handicap, Impede, Obstruct, Prevent, Restrain, Thwart, Hold up

Antonyms: Aid, Assist, Host, Encourage, Expedite, Forward, Further, Help, Promote, Speed

Handy

(Adjective)

Synonyms: Skilled, Skilful, Accessible, Available, Useful, Adopt, Expert, Adroit, Proficient, Dexterous, Ready, Close, Near, Convenient

Antonyms: Unskilled, Unskillful, Bungling, Clumsy, Unhandy, Awkward, Inept, Maladroit, Useless

Handle
(Verb)

Synonyms: Hold, Wield, Touch, Carry out
Antonyms: Throw, Bungle, Miscarry

Hard
(Adjective)

Synonyms: Arduous, Difficult, Laborious, Troublesome, Trying
Antonyms: Easy, Simple, Plain, Flexible, Malleable, Pliable, Weak, Soft

Harsh
(Adjective)

Synonyms: Jarring, Rancorous, Discordant, Strident
Antonyms: Musical, Concordant, Tuneful, Melodious, Mild

Hate
(Verb)

Synonyms: Abhor, Abominate, Be hostile to, Be repelled by, Be sick of, Despise, Dislike, Have an aversion to, Loath, Be reluctant, Shrink from
Antonyms: Be fond of, Cherish, Dote on, Enjoy, Esteem, Fancy, Like, Love, Relish, Treasure, Wish

Hazard
(Noun)

Synonyms: Accident, Chance, Danger, Jeopardy, Risk, Venture, Peril, Contingency, Threat
Antonyms: Assurance, Certainty, Necessity, Protection, Safeguard, Security, Surety

Healthy
(Adjective)

Synonyms: Hygienic, Sanitary, Well, Wholesome, Vigorous, Strong, Robust, Sound, Hale, Hearty, Sound, Sturdy

Antonyms: Wasted, Worn, Failing exhausted, Sick, Sickly, Ill, Unhealthy, Weak, Weakly, Unsound

Hesitate
(Verb)

Synonyms: Waver, Tarry, Totter, Pause, Demur, Falter, Vacillate
Antonyms: Determine, Settle, End, Decide, Resolve

Heavy
(Adjective)

Synonyms: Crushing, Burdensome, Onerous, Oppressing, Sluggish, Gloomy, Serious, Difficult
Antonyms: Trivial, Easy, Light, Mild, Agile, Bearable, Gentle

High
(Adjective)

Synonyms: Elevated, Exalted, Noble, Tall, Lofty, Towering, Steep, Soaring, Great
Antonyms: Deep, Base, Low, Short, Degraded, Drafted, Stunted, Mild

High
(Adjective)

Synonyms: Elevated, Tall, Lofty, Towering, Steep, Soaring, Great,
Antonyms: Base, Low, Short, Degraded, Drafted, Stunted, Mild

Hire
(Verb)

Synonyms: Engage, Employ, Appoint, Commission, Lease, Charge, Rent, Enlist, Recruit
Antonyms: Purchase, Buy, Fire, Retire, Discharge

Holy
(Adjective)

Synonyms: Religious, Godly, Pious, Pure, Sublime, Virtuous, Saintly, Sacred, Hallowed, Divine

Antonyms: Irreligious, Ungodly, Irreverent, Blasphemous, Wicked, Unholy, Sacrilegious, Profane

Horrible
(Adjective)

Synonyms: Frightful, Appalling, Dire, Ghastly, Ugly, Fearful, Awful, Terrific, Dreadful, Hideous, Repulsive
Antonyms: Agreeable, Pleasant, Delightful, Pleasurable, Charming, Pleasing

Hot
(Adjective)

Synonyms: Burning, Feverish, Scorching, Torrid
Antonyms: Cold, Cool, Calm, Soothing

Humane
(Adjective)

Synonyms: Humanitarian, Philanthropic, Sympathetic, Tender, Kind, Benign, Human, Charitable, Compassionate
Antonyms: Inhuman, Unkind, Cruel, Uncharitable, Malignant

Humid
(Adjective)

Synonyms: Wet, Moist, Close, Sticky, Oppressive
Antonyms: Parched, Dry, Arid, Sunny, Torrid

Humor
(Noun)

Synonyms: Wit, Fun, Comedy, Factiousness, Amusement, Jocularity, Pleasantry
Antonyms: Solemnity, Gravity, Sobriety, Seriousness

Humorous
(Adjective)

Synonyms: Funny, Witty, Comic, Comical, Droll, Jocose, Jocular, Waggish
Antonyms: Serious, Grave, Dull, Sedate, Gloomy

Hypocrisy

(Noun)

Synonyms: Deceit, Dissembling, Duplicity, Pretence, Falsify, Deception, Cant

Antonyms: Honesty, Uprightness, Straightforwardness, Sincerity, Truthfulness,

I

Icy

(Adjective)

Synonyms: Arctic, Hitting, Bitter, Chill, Chilling, Chilly, Freezing, Aloof, Cold, Distant, Forbidding, Frigid, Frosty, Glacial, Indifferent, Stony

Antonyms: Blistering, Boiling, Not sizzling, Cordial, Friendly, Gracious, Warm

Idea

(Noun)

Synonyms: Supposition, Thought, Opinion, Imagination, Conception, Doctrine, Impression

Antonyms: Truth, Actuality, Fact, Reality, Verity

Ideal

(Adjective)

Synonyms : Archetype, Model, Prototype, Example, Standard, Original, Pattern

Antonyms: Factual, Realistic, Practical, Deficient, Impaired, Imperfect, Unsuitable

Identical

(Adjective)

Synonyms : Alike, Synonymous, Tantamount, Interchangeable, Self-same, Equivalent

Antonyms: Different, Opposite, Contrast, Autonymous

Idle

(Adjective)

Synonyms: Inert, Unoccupied, Lazy, Inactive, Sloth, Sluggish, Unemployed, Indolent

Antonyms: Active, Busy, Diligent, Industrious, Assiduous

Ignorance

(Noun)

Synonyms: Illiteracy, Unexplored, Simplicity, Blindness, Darkness, Soil, Ground, Simpleness

Antonyms: Acquaintance, Wisdom, Light, Intelligence

Image

(Noun)

Synonyms: Resemblance, Effigy, Statue, Picture, Likeness, Representation

Antonyms: Unidentical, Contrast, Contradictory

Imitate

(Verb)

Synonyms: Burlesque, Echo, Follow, Copy, Impersonate, Mock, Mimic, Counterfeit, Forge, Parody

Antonyms: Alter, Convert, Modify, Vary

Immediately

(Adjective)

Synonyms: At once, Now right off, Without delay, Right away, Intantly, Instant

Antonyms : After a while, In future, By and by, Hereafter

Imminent

(Adjective)

Synonyms: Impending, Threatening

Antonyms : Chimerical, Problematical, Improbable, Unlikely, Doubtful, Contingent

Impartial

(Adjective)

Synonyms: Neutral, Just, Unbiased, Fair Equitable

Antonyms : Partial, Unfair, Biased, Prejudiced

Impertinence

(Noun)

Synonyms: Assurance, Boldness, Forwardness, Sauciness, Insolence, Incivility, Impudence, Presumption

Antonyms : Bashfulness, Coyness, Submissiveness, Modesty, Meekness, Diffidence

Importance

(Noun)

Synonyms: Important, Significance, Moment, Mark, Primacy, Greatness, Superiority, Distinction, Concern

Antonyms : Unimportance, Insignificance, Pettines, Purpoeleseness, Meanness

Important

(Adjective)

Synonyms: Consequential, Great, Prominent, Weighty, Serious, Relevant, Powerful, Prominent, Materil, Essential, Grave, Momentous

Antonyms : Feeble, Flimsy, Worthless, Ueless, Nonessential, Slight, Secondary, Incosiderable, Idle

Impossible

(Adjective)

Synonyms: Absurd, Unreasonable, Out of reach Out of question, Impracticable, Incredible, Hopeless

Antonyms : Possible, Probable, Practical

Improve

(Verb)

Synonyms: Increase, Amend, Correct, Reform, Rectify, Ameliorate, Better

Antonyms: Spoil, Deteriorate, Corrupt, Mar, Damage, Deprecate, Impair

Imprudent
(Adjective)

Synonyms: Careless, Fool hardy, Foolish, Headless, Ill-advised, Ill-considered, Ill-judged, Improvident, Irresponsible, Rash, Reckless

Antonyms : Careful, Cautions, Considerate, Discreet, Judicious, Polite, Provident, Prudent, Responsible, Wise

Incapable
(Adjective)

Synonyms: Incompetent, Inefficient, Unqualified, Inadequate, Unable, Unfit, Disabled

Antonyms: Gifted, Capable, Qualified, Accomplished, Competent, Efficient

Inclement
(Adjective)

Synonyms: Rough, Stormy, Rigorous, Severe, Harsh, Draconian, Unfavorable, Unpleasant

Antonyms: Genial, Mild, Pleasant, Favorable, Balmy, Clement, Merciful

Incline
(Verb)

Synonyms: Dispose, Lean, Fall upon, Tend towards, Slope

Antonyms: Indispose, Rise, Go upwards, Repel

Include
(Verb)

Synonyms : Involve, Comprise, Contain, Comprehend

Antonyms: Exclude, Omit, Leave out

Inconsistent
(Adjective)

Synonyms: Capricious, Erratic, Fickle, Changeable, Irregular,

Uneven, Unstable, Contradictory, Contrary, At variance, Conflicting, Inconstant
Antonyms: Consistent, Constant, Predictable, Reliable, Stable, Steady, Coherent, Homogeneous, Orderly, Uniform, Reconcilable

Incur
(Verb)
Synonyms: Run, Meet, Bring, Danger, Blame, Expose, Gain, Contract, Induce
Antonyms: Shun, Avoid, Escape, Defect

Indecent
(Adjective)
Synonyms: Indelicate, Lewd, Indecorous, Unchaste, Improper, Shameless, Filthy, Foul
Antonyms: Decent, Seemly, Pure, Moral, Proper, Virtuous, Chaste, Decorous

Induce
(Verb)
Synonyms: Impel, Convince, Instigate, Generate, Persuade, Cajole, Urge, Coax, Wheedle, Move
Antonyms: Hinder, Repel, Curb, Deter, Prevent, Restrain, Discourage, Subdue

Influence
(Noun)
Synonyms: Actuate, Draw, Excite, Inflame, Lead, Prompt, Urge, Move, Induce, Stir, Drive, Incite, Compel
Antonyms: Retard, Dissuade, Hinder, Deter, Prevent, Inhibit, Restrain

Inner
(Adjective)
Synonyms: Inward, Interior, Internal, Real
Antonyms: Outer, Exterior, External, Superficial

Innocent
(Adjective)
Synonyms: Blameless, Sinless, Untainted, Virginal, Guiltless, Irreproachable,
Antonyms: Blameworthy, Culpable, Guilty, Immoral, Lewd, Impure, Unchaste, Depraved, Dirty, Indecent

Insert
(Verb)
Synonyms: Introduce, Interpose, Infix, Interject, Interpolate
Antonyms: Abstract, Excerpt, Extract, Detach, Release, Remove

Insist
(Verb)
Synonyms: Urge, Persist, Contend, Demand, Maintain, Preserve
Antonyms: Relinquish, Forgo, Waiver, Renounce, Abandon

Integrity
(Noun)
Synonyms: Honesty, Probity, Sincerity, Truthfulness, Rectitude, Truth
Antonyms: Unfairness, Dishonesty, Disunity, Diversity

Intensify
(Verb)
Synonyms: Aggravate, Heighten, Magnify, Increase, Enhance
Antonyms: Milden, Lessen, Diminish, Attenuate, Reduce, Alleviate, Assuage

Invincible
(Adjective)
Synonyms: Impregnable, Indestructible, Indomitable, Inseparable, Insuperable, Invulnerable, Unassailable, Unconquerable, Insurmountable
Antonyms: Assailable, Beatable, Conquerable, Defenseless, Fallible, Powerless, Unprotected, Vulnerable, Weak, Yielding

J

Jaundiced
(Adjective)

Synonyms: Cynical, Preconceived, Skeptical, Bitter, Biased, Distorted, Envious, Hostile, Jealous, Partial, Prejudiced, Resentful, Spiteful, Suspicious
Antonyms: Credulous, Ingenuous, Naive, Optimistic, Open-minded, Trusting, Unbiased

Jealous
(Adjective)

Synonyms: Envious, Suspicious, Covetous
Antonyms: Indifferent, Genital, Liberal

Jest
(Noun)

Synonyms: Fun, Joke, Jeer, Taunt, Amuse
Antonyms: Seriousness, Thoughtful, Earnest, Sober

Jesting
(Adjective)

Synonyms: Aping, Humour, Joking, Playing the fool, Clowning, Jocularity
Antonyms: Seriousness, Businessmanship, Tragedy, Gravity

Journey
(Noun)

Synonyms: Tour, Passage, Travel, Cruise, Expedition, Transit, Trip, Voyage
Antonyms: Stability, Established, Settled

Joyous
(Adjective)
Synonyms: Ecstatic, Elated, Jovial, Genial, Jolly, Glad, Happy
Antonyms: Gloomy, Miserable, Morose, Solemn, Sad, Unhappy

Judge
(Adjective)
Synonyms: Justice, Umpire, Jurist, Justice court, Arbiter
Antonyms: Commander, Dictator, Critic, Self-server

Jump
(Adjective)
Synonyms: Bound, Spring, Cape, Bounce, Vault, Skip, Leap
Antonyms: Sink, Fall, Drop

Just
(Adjective)
Synonyms: Decent, Fair, Good, Honest, Impartial, Pure, Right, Accurate, Exact, Faithful, Lawful, Apt, Deserved, Proper, Suitable, Legitimate
Antonyms: Corrupt, Devious, Dishonest, Inequitable, Prejudiced, Unfair, Unjust, Unlawful, Untrue, Inappropriate, Undeserved, Unfit

Justify
(Verb)
Synonyms: Absolve, Defend, Clear, Explain, Perform
Antonyms: Condemn, Accuse, Censure, Blame, Denounce

K

Keen
(Adjective)
Synonyms: Acute, Eager, Sharp, Shrewd, Penetrating
Antonyms: Slow, Stupid, Bland, Languid, Dull, Indifferent

Kill
(Verb)
Synonyms: Assimilate, Dispatch, Massacre, Murder, Slaughter, Put to death, Butcher, Execute
Antonyms: Originate, Create, Produce, Fashion, Cause

Kind
(Adjective)
Synonyms: Compassionate, Benign, Affable, Generous, Lenient, Sympathetic, Charitable, Merciful, Tender, Philanthropic, Complacent
Antonyms: Cruel, Callous, Unfeeling, Unkind, Hard, Hearted, Insensible, Harsh

Kindle
(Verb)
Synonyms: Ignite, Inflame, Light, Fire, Agitate, Excite, Incite, Induce
Antonyms: Extinguish, Put out, Satisfy, Satiate

Knowledge
(Noun)
Synonyms: Perception, Science, Wisdom, Intuition, Comprehension, Cognition, Information, Lore, Light,

Intelligence
Antonyms: Ignorance, Unfamiliarity, Misunderstanding, Misapprehension, Inexperience, Illiteracy

Known

(Adjective)

Synonyms: Acknowledged, Admitted, Avowed, Celebrated, Common, Familiar, Manifest, Obvious, Patent, Popular, Published, Recognized, Well-known
Antonyms: Closet, Concealed, Hidden, Secret, Unfamiliar, Unknown, Unrecognized, Unrevealed

L

Labor
(Noun)
Synonyms: Work, Toil, Exertion, Drudgery, Industry
Antonyms: Repose, Rest, Relaxation, Stillness

Lack
(Noun)
Synonyms: Need, Shortage, Deficiency, Want
Antonyms: Sufficiency, Prosperity, Wealth, Riches

Large
(Adjective)
Synonyms: Big, Mammoth, Great, Monumental
Antonyms: Small, Minute, Delicate, Sophisticated

Lawful
(Adjective)
Synonyms: Rightful, Legal, Fair, Legitimate
Antonyms: Illegal, Unlawful, Illicit, Banned, Forbidden

Lazy
(Adjective)
Synonyms: Idle, Sluggish, Indolent, Unemployed, Slow, Slothful, Delinquent
Antonyms: Active, Smart, Agile, Up and doing

Leader
(Noun)
Synonyms: Guide, Guru, Teacher, Director, Conductor, Principal, Politician

Antonym s: Follower, Trainee, Apprentice, Pupil, Henchman

Learn

(Verb)

Synonyms: Acquire, Memorize, Discover, Attain, Imbibe, Detect, Trace

Antonyms: Forget, Unlearn, Miss, Misunderstand, Ignore

Learning

(Noun)

Synonyms: Scholarship, Erudition, Knowledge, Understanding

Antonyms : Ignorance, Illiteracy, Misunderstanding, Unlearning

Lengthy

(Adjective)

Synonyms: Tedious, Diffused, Detailed, Prolix, Spread

Antonyms: Short, Concise, Brief, Limited, Terse

Lessen

(Noun)

Synonyms: Lighten, Assuage, Allay, Mitigate, Soften, Temper

Antonyms: Heighten, Toughen, Enlarge, Escalate, Extend, Intensify

Liberal

(Adjective)

Synonyms: Plentiful, Tolerant, Profuse, Free, Progressive, Generous, Flexible

Antonyms: Scanty, Grasping, Low, Mean

Liberty

(Noun)

Synonyms: Emancipation, Freedom, Independence, Licence, Permission

Antonyms: Captivity, Compulsion, Constraint, Imprisonment, Slavery, Serfdom, Servitude, Oppression, Obligation, Thraldom

Lie
(Noun)

Synonyms: Falsehood, Untruth, Prevarication, Quibble, Practice, Collusion
Antonyms: Truth, Honesty, Veracity, Authenticity, Original

Lift
(Verb)

Synonyms: Exalt, Erect, Raise, Elevate, Hoist
Antonyms : Drop, Lower, Sink, Let, Fall

Likely
(Adjective)

Synonyms: Conjectural, Apt, Reasonable, Presumable, Liable, Credible, Possible, Conceivable
Antonyms: Doubtful, Improbable, Questionable, Unlikely, Dubious, Unreasonable

Lively
(Adjective)

Synonyms: Vivid, Vigorous, Brisk, Keen, Vivacious, Spirited
Antonyms: Listless, Languid, Languorous, Lethargic, Lifeless, Immobile

Lonely
(Adjective)

Synonyms: Solitary, Desolate, Isolated, Deserted, Alone, Single
Antonyms: Escorted, Attended, Befriended, Popular, Together, Accompanied

Lock
(Verb)

Synonyms: Behold, Inspect, See, Watch, View, Stare, Gaze, Discern, Observe, Regard, Survey, Arrest
Antonyms: Ignore, Reject, Veil, Bypass

Loud
(Adjective)

Synonyms: Noisy, Vociferous, Clamorous, Boisterous, Sound

Antonyms: Peaceful, Silent, Soft, Taciturn, Subdued

Love
(Noun)

Synonyms: Affection, Fondness, Charity, Liking, Regard, Friendship, Tenderness, Attraction
Antonyms: Dislike, Abhorrence, Animosity, Disgust, Repugnance, Antipathy, Abomination, Loathing, Aversion, Detestation

Luck
(Noun)

Synonyms: Fortune, Chance, Prosperity, Good, Stroke
Antonyms: Bad luck, Misfortune, Bad stroke, Unfavorable, Loss, Missing

Loving
(Adjective)

Synonyms: Affectionate, Devoted, Fond, Ardent, Dear, Solicitors
Antonyms: Bitter, Cold, Unaffectionate, Aloof, Cruel, Hostile, Mean

M

Magnanimous

(Adjective)

Synonyms: Beneficent, Big, Bountiful, Charitable, Free, Handsome, Kind, Noble, Beneficent, Selfless

Antonyms: Miserly, Petty, Resentful, Selfish, Small, Unforgiving, Vindictive

Magnetic

(Adjective)

Synonyms: Alluring, Captivating, Charismatic, Charming, Enchanting, Fascinating, Hypnotic, Irresistible, Mesmerizing, Seductive

Antonyms: Disagreeable, Offensive, Repellent, Repulsive, Unattractive, Unlikable, Unpleasant

Magnificent

(Adjective)

Synonyms: August, Elegant, Glorious, Grand, Impressive, Lavish, Luxurious, Majestic, Opulent, Rich, Regal, Sublime, Transcendent

Antonyms: Bad, Humble, Ignoble, Lowly, Mean, Modest, Ordinary, Petty, Poor, Trivial, Undistinguished, Unimposing

Maintain

(Verb)

Synonyms: Carry on, Conserve, Keep, Nurture, Retain, Uphold, Support, Claim, Contend, Justify, Vindicate, Perpetuate

Antonyms: Abolish, Break off, Conclude, Drop, End, Give up, Relinquish, Abandon, Suspend, Terminate, Desert

Majority
(Noun)

Synonyms: Adulthood, Excess, Superiority, Preponderance, More than half

Antonyms: Minority, Smallness, Inferiority

Manner
(Noun)

Synonyms: Style, Mode, Custom, Method, System, Way, Fashion, Conduct, Behavior

Antonyms: Mannerlessness, Discourteous, Unsocial,Unsystematic, Unmethodical

Melody
(Noun)

Synonyms: Unison, Tune, Symphony, Music, Harmony, Air

Antonyms: Discord, Distortion, Disruption, Noise

Mercy
(Noun)

Synonyms: Benevolence, Favour, Pardon, Clemency, Compassion, Gentleness, Leniency, Pity, Mildness, Grace, Kindness

Antonyms: Cruelty, Hardness, Harshness, Vigor, Severity, Penalty, Punishment

Merit
(Noun)

Synonyms: Worth, Value, Excellence, Virtue

Antonyms: Fault, Error, Flaw, Weakness, Worthlessness

Mild
(Adjective)

Synonyms: Bland, Soft, Gentle, Kind, Docile, Tender, Meek, Placid

Antonyms: Wild, Ferocious, Bloodthirsty, Fierce, Brutish, Savage

Mind
(Noun)

Synonyms: Wit, Thought, Sense, Reason, Intellect, Disposition, Brian, Intelligence, Understanding, Spirit
Antonyms: Body, Matter, Brown, Brute force, Material, Substance

Miscellaneous
(Adjective)

Synonyms: Mixed, Assorted, Mingled, Motley, Unlike, Various, Variant, Dissimilar, Discordant, Confused, Promiscuous
Antonyms: Homogeneous, Identical, Like, Pure, Uniform, Same, Similar

Miserable
(Adjective)

Synonyms: Forlorn, Unhappy, Dismal, Sorry, Wretched
Antonyms: Happy, Cheerful, Joyous, Contended,

Misery
(Noun)

Synonyms: Woe, Wretchedness, Heartache, Distress, Anguish, Torment, Torture, Agony, Discomfort
Antonyms: Bliss, Joy, Happiness, Pleasure, Ecstasy, Elation, Sweetness

Mislead
(Verb)

Synonyms: Misguide, Deceive, Delude, Misdirect, Beguile, Mislead
Antonyms: Pilot, Guide, Direct, Steer, Lead

Modern
(Adjective)

Synonyms: Novel, New, Present, Contemporary, Current,

Recent, Timely, Present day
Antonyms: Bygone, Past, Ancient, Old fashioned

Modest
(Adjective)

Synonyms: Lowly, Humble, Shy, Unassuming, Unpretentious
Antonyms: Conceited, Pretentious, Showy, Overbearing, Immodest

Monotonous
(Adjective)

Synonyms: All the same, Boring, Colorless, Droning, Dull, Flat, Humdrum, Plodding, Repetitive, Soporific, Tiresome, Unchanging, Uniform, Wearisome
Antonyms: Animated, Enjoyable, Entertaining, Enthralling, Exciting, Exhilarating, Interesting, Lively, Invigorating

Moral
(Adjective)

Synonyms: Honorable, Upright, Just, Fair, Ethical, Strict, Right, Virtuous
Antonyms: Immoral, Dishonorable, Vicious, Licentious, Unprincipled, Unrighteous

Mourn
(Verb)

Synonyms: Bemoan, Bewail, Sorrow, Lament, Regret, Grieve, Deplore, Cry
Antonyms: Be joyful, Joy, Rejoice, Triumph, Enjoy, Please

Mysterious
(Adjective)

Synonyms: Abstruse, Arcane, Cryptic, Curious, Enigmatic, Hidden, Obscure, Perplexing, Puzzling, Secret, Unknown, Veiled
Antonyms: Apparent, Clear, Manifest, Open, Plain

N

Native

(Adjective & Noun)

Synonyms: Aboriginals, Innate, Natal, Original, Natural, Indigenous

Antonyms: Foreign, Extraneous, Alien, Acquired, Supplemented, Extrinsic

Necessary

(Adjective)

Synonyms: Essential, Needful, Required, Requisite, Undeniable, Unavoidable

Antonyms: Casual, Worthless, Needless, Non Essential, Optional, Unnecessary, Useless

Neglect

(Noun)

Synonyms: Carelessness, Neglectfulness, Negligence, Omission, Oversight, Slight, Scorn, Slackness, Inadvertence, Heedlessness, Default, Failure, Disregard, Disrespect, Error

Antonyms: Care, Attention, Observation, Adventure, Heed

Nervous

(Adjective)

Synonyms: Hesitant, Shaky, Timid, Timorous, Afraid, Agitated

Antonyms: Courageous, Bold, Manly, Undaunted, Doughtily, Valiant, Brave,

New
(Adjective)

Synonyms: Unused, Fresh, Novel, Recent, Modern
Antonyms: Old, Ancient, Aged, Obsolete, Antique, Antiquated

Nimble
(Adjective)

Synonyms: Active, Agile, Prompt, Flexible, Quick, Speedy, Spry, Swift
Antonyms: Clumsy, Unready, Sluggish, Inert, Inactive, Dull, Dilatory

Noble
(Adjective)

Synonyms: Dignified, Lofty, Eminent, Honorable, Magnificent, Great, Illustrious, Elevated, Peer, Lord, Aristocrat, Grand
Antonyms: Ignoble, Mean, Humble, Common, Plebeian

Notion
(Noun)

Synonyms: Conception, Impression, Imagination, Opinion, Doctrine, Belief, Supposition, Thought
Antonyms: Truth, Reality, Fact, Variety, Actuality

Numerous
(Adjective)

Synonyms: Various, Several, Manifold, Sundry, Diverse
Antonyms: Few, Scarce, Scanty, Rare

O

Obdurate
(Adjective)

Synonyms: Adamant, Dogged, Firm, Fixed, Hard, Hard-hearted, Immovable, Inexorable, Inflexible, Obstinate, Relentless, Unending, Inexpressible

Antonyms: Amenable, Biddable, Complaint, Flexible, Malleable, Plaint, Soft-hearted, Submissive, Tender, Tractable, Yielding, Placid

Obedient
(Adjective)

Synonyms: Submissive, Subservient, Dutiful, Tractable, Yielding

Antonyms: Mutinous, Stubborn, Intractable, Disobedient, Refractor

Obligatory
(Adjective)

Synonyms: Necessary, Unavoidable, Needful, Imperative, Compulsory

Antonyms: Desired, Willing, Voluntary, Self, Chosen

Obliterate
(Verb)

Synonyms: Annihilate, Blot out, Cancel, Destroy, Efface, Eradicate, Erase, Expunge, Extirpate, Root out, Wipe out

Antonyms: Build, Construct, Create, Establish, Form, Formulate, Generate, Make

Oblivious
(Adjective)
Synonyms: Forgetful, Absent - minded, Inattentive
Antonyms: Attentive, Aware, Observant

Obvious
.(Adjective)
Synonyms: Clear, Evident, Visible, Distinct, Palpable, Patent, Discernible, Perceptible
Antonyms: Hidden, Masked, Veiled, Covered, Secret, Obscure, Concealed, Latent

Obscure
(Adjective)
Synonyms: Dark, Doubtful, Dim, Dense, Hidden, Dusky, Muddy, Turbid, Involved, Unintelligent, Deep, Darksome, Cloudy
Antonyms: Apparent, Intelligible, Lucid, Plain, Straightforward, Transparent, Unadorned, Obvious, Evident, Distinct

Odd
(Adjective)
Synonyms: Queer, Uneven, Uninvited, Irregular
Antonyms: Usual, Match, Matching, Even, Parallel

Odious
(Adjective)
Synonyms: Abhorrent, Abominable, Detestable, Disgusting, Execrable, Foul, Hateful, Horrible, Horrid, Loathsome, Obnoxious, Repugnant, Repulsive, Unpleasant, Vile
Antonyms: Agreeable, Charming, Congenial, Delightful, Enchanting, Enjoyable, Pleasant, Pleasing, Winsome

Onerous
(Adjective)
Synonyms: Burdensome, Troublesome, Backbreaking, Wearing, Oppressive, Difficult
Antonyms: Easy, Fluent, Harmless, Comfortable

Ooze
(Verb)
Synonyms: Drip, Drop, Drizzle, Let fall
Antonyms: Rush, Pour, Gush, Flow, Rain

Opinion
(Noun)
Synonyms: Bar, Combat, Thought, Idea, Judgment, Theory, Dogma, Tenet, Mind, Notion, Speculation, Verdict
Antonyms: Aid, Abet, Silence, Dictation, Non-committal, Execution, Order

Opportunity
(Noun)
Synonyms: Chance, Occasion, Turn, Scope, Window, Expedient
Antonyms: Omission, Lapse, Neglect, Leave undone

Optimistic
(Adjective)
Synonyms: Hopeful, Confident, Brave, Bright, Cheerful, Happy
Antonyms: Pessimist, Dejected, Drooping, Disappointment, Cheerless, Hopeless

Opulent
(Adjective)
Synonyms: Affluent, Lavish, Luxurious, Moneyed, Prosperous, Sumptuous, Wealthy, Well-to-do, Copious, Plentiful, Profuse, Prolific
Antonyms: Destitute, Down and out, Broke, Moneyless, Needy, Penurious, Poor, Poverty – stricken

Orderly
(Adjective)
Synonyms: Neat, Tidy, Trim, Uniform, Graceful
Antonyms: Chaotic, Disorderly, Untidy, Messy

Ordinary
(Adjective)
Synonyms: Average, Common, Usual, Commonplace, Regular, Medium, Low, Inferior, Undistinguished
Antonyms: Extraordinary, One-in-a-million, Uncommon, Above the average, Abnormally high, First rate, Superior, Distinguished

Organize
(Verb)
Synonyms: Classify, Arrange, Order, Sort, Marshal
Antonyms: Disorganize, Muddle, Bungle, Dishevel

Original
(Adjective)
Synonyms: Aboriginal, Earliest, Initial, Introductory, Primary, Primitive, Fresh, Novel, Fertile, Inventive, First, Genuine, Authentic, Master, Prototypical,
Antonyms: Final, Last, Antiquated, Conventional, Familiar, Normal, Old, Ordinary, Spoiled, Standard, Traditional, Typical, Usual, Secondary

Outbreak
(Noun)
Synonyms: Commotion, Tumult, Insurrection, Outburst
Antonyms: Order, Quiet, Subsidence, Peace

Outstanding
(Adjective)
Synonyms: Celebrated, Distinguished, Eminent, Great, Important, Impressive, Special, Superior, Superlative, Due, Payable, Arresting, Eye-catching, Prominent, Salient
Antonyms: Dull, Inferior, Insignificant, Mediocre, Ordinary, Pedestrian, Run of the mill, Unexceptional, Unimpressive

P

Pacify

(Verb)

Synonyms: Appease, Mitigate, Quench, Lull, Allay, Compose, Quiet, Assuage, Tranquillize

Antonyms: Irritate, Inflame, Annoy, Incense, Enrage, Exasperate, Vex

Pain

(Noun)

Synonyms: Distress, Torment, Woe, Twinge, Throe, Pang, Ache, Grief, Distress, Throb, Agony

Antonyms: Comfort, Ease, Peace, Health, Pleasure, Well-being, Ecstasy, Relief

Pardon

(Verb)

Synonyms: Pass by, Remit, Pass over, Condone, Forgive, Absolve, Exonerate, Acquit, Excuse, Overlook

Antonyms: Castigate, Chasten, Visit, Sentence, Doom, Condemn, Convict, Punish, Penalize

Pardon

(Noun)

Synonyms: Oblivion, Absolution, Mercy, Remission, Amnesty, Forgiveness, Acquittal

Antonyms: Penalty, Retaliation, Punishment, Retribution, Vengeance

Part
(Noun)
Synonyms: Atom, Member, Portion, Share, Segment, Section, Particle, Fraction, Fragment, Piece, Disconnect, Disjoin
Antonyms: Connect, Join, Tie, Attach, Link, Combine, Couple, Cement

Partial
(Adjective)
Synonyms: Unfair, Incomplete, Limited, Biased, Inequitable, Restricted, Predisposed, One-sided
Antonyms: Fair, Complete, Entire, Equitable, Disinterested, Whole, Just, Impartial

Passion
(Noun)
Synonyms: Love, Anger, Fury, Emotion, Fever, Desire, Excitement, Zeal, Fervor
Antonyms: Apathy, Calmness, Coolness, Hate, Indifference, Frigidity, Unconcern

Passive
(Adjective)
Synonyms: Patient, Inert, Submissive, Resistant
Antonyms: Active, Alert, Vigilant, Watchful

Paternal
(Adjective)
Synonyms: Careful, Fatherly, Patronizing, Kind-Hearted
Antonyms: Careless, Rough, Rude, Indifferent

Patience
(Noun)
Synonyms: Forbearance, Passiveness, Sufferance, Resignation, Endurance, Fortitude, Calmness
Antonyms: Wrath, Enrage, Enjoy, Infuriate, Vex, Displease, Inflame, Incite, Indignation, Irritation

Pause
(Noun)
Synonyms: Respite, Interval, Break, Halt, Cessation, Intermission, Lull, Suspension, Stoppage, Wait
Antonyms: Continue, Continuance, Continuation, Continuity

Peculiar
(Adjective)
Synonyms: Strange, Extraordinary, Remarkable, Odd, Queer, Unusual, Rare, Abnormal, Uncommon, Irregular, Singular
Antonyms: Natural, Customary, Normal, Commonplace, Usual, Ordinary

Peevish
(Adjective)
Synonyms: Acrimonious, Cantankerous, Captions, Childish, Churlish, Crusty, Fractions, Fretful, Ill-tempered, Petulant, Sulky, Sullen, Surly, Testy, Tetehy, Touchy
Antonyms: Affable, Agreeable, Cheerful, Cheery, Easy-Going, Even – tempered, Genial, Good- natured, Happy, Merry, Pleasant, Sweet

Perfect
(Adjective)
Synonyms: Flawless, Faultless, Ideal, Consummation
Antonyms: Deficient, Imperfect, Flawed, Incomplete, Unfinished, Defective

Permanent
(Adjective)
Synonyms: Stable, Enduring, Constant, Everlasting, Steadfast, Lasting, Durable
Antonyms: Brief, Temporary, Short- lived, Changing, Mortal, Transitory

Permission
(Noun)
Synonym: Allowance, Leave, License, Permit, Liberty, Authority,

Consent
Antonyms: Prevention, Refusal, Resistance, Prohibition, Denial, Hindrance, Opposition, Objection

Permit
(Verb)
Synonyms: Let, Allow, Agree, Authorize, Enable
Antonyms: Forbid, Prevent, Prohibit

Persist
(Verb)
Synonyms: Continue, Last, Remain, Stay, Endure, Insist, Preserve
Antonyms: Discontinue, Conclude, Quit, Finish, Terminate, End, Desist, Cease

Persistent
(Adjective)
Synonyms: Ceaseless, Continuous, Unceasing, Unremitting
Antonyms: Occasional, Periodic, Inconstant, Changeable, Temporary

Persuade
(Verb)
Synonyms: Allure, Urge, Lead, Incite, Entice, Coax, Convince, Incline, Move, Induce, Impel, Bring
Antonyms: Hold back, Restrain, Deter, Repel, Dissuade, Hinder, Discourage

Physical
(Adjective)
Synonyms: Bodily, Carnal, Corporal, Somatic, Real, Visible
Antonyms: Mental, Spiritual, Intellectual

Pitiable
(Adjective)
Synonyms: Mournful, Moving, Grievous, Distressing, Sad, Doleful, Woeful, Sorrowful

Antonyms: Pleasant, Desirable, Enviable

Placid

(Adjective)

Synonyms: Calm, Collected, Composed, Cool, Even, Gently, Halcyon, Mild, Peaceful, Serene, Still, Tranquil, Undisturbed, Unexcitable, Untroubled

Antonyms: Agitated, Disturbed, Emotional, Excitable, Impulsive, Passionate, Rough, Temperamental, Tempestuous

Plain

(Adjective)

Synonyms: Clear, Evident, Obvious, Conspicuous, Apparent

Antonyms: Hidden, Concealed, Secret, Imperceptible

Plead

(Verb)

Synonyms: Pray, Sue, Supplicate, Entreat

Antonyms: Command, Demand, Order,

Pleasant

(Adjective)

Synonyms: Delicious, Gratifying, Pleasing, Agreeable, Attractive, Enjoyable, Nice

Antonyms: Arrogant, Awful, Distasteful, Displeasing, Unpleasant, Repulsive, Unattractive, Obnoxious

Pleasure

(Noun)

Synonyms: Delight, Enjoyment, Joy, Ecstasy

Antonyms: Awful, Distasteful, Displeasing, Unpleasant, Repulsive, Unattractive, Obnoxious

Plentiful

(Adjective)

Synonyms: Abundant, Lavish, Replete, Luxuriant, Bountiful, Ample, Plenteous, Teeming, Sufficient

Antonyms: Scarce, Limited, Niggardly, Sparing, Skimpy, Scanty, Insufficient

Polished

(Adjective)

Synonyms: Accomplished, Adept, Faultless, Fine, Impeccable, Skillful, Bright, Gleaming, Glossy, Cultivated, Finished, Polite, Sophisticated, Refined, Shining, Elegant, Perfect, Pleasant

Antonyms: Amateurish, Inept, Inexpert, Dark, Dull, Matt, Rough, Uncivilized, Uncultivated, Unrefined, Crude, Unskilled, Unpolished

Polite

(Adjective)

Synonyms: Elegant, Polished, Urbane, Genteel, Gallant, Courtly, Courteous, Civil, Complaisance, Chivalrous, Cultivated

Antonyms: Awkward, Bluff, Untaught, Unpolished, Uncouth, Brusque, Ill-bred, Clownish, Raw, Insolent, Insulting, Discourteous

Poor

(Adjective)

Synonyms: Hard up, Destitute, Meager, Unfortunate, Inferior, Under-privileged, Ordinary

Antonyms: Rich, Privilege, Excellent, Fortunate, Happy, Extraordinary

Possess

(Verb)

Synonyms: Have, Command, Seize, Own, Hold, Obtain, Enjoy

Antonyms: Want, Forfeit, Lose, Need, Dispose, Relinquish

Possible

(Adjective)

Synonyms: Likely, Potential, Conceivable, Practicable, Feasible

Antonyms: Impossible, Incredible, Unfeasible, Impracticable, Unachievable, Inconceivable

Praise
(Verb)

Synonyms: Acclaim, Flattery, Plaudits, Laudation, Approval, Cheers, Cheering, Compliment, Applause, Approbation
Antonyms: Abuse, Vituperation, Slander, Scorn, Repudiation, Obloquy, Reproof, Hissing, Disparagement, Contempt, Blame, Condemnation, Slander-Mongering

Precarious
(Adjective)

Synonyms: Doubtful, Dubious, Hairy, Hazardous, Insecure, Perilous, Risky, Shaky, Slippery, Touch and go, Tricky, Uncertain, Unreliable, Unsafe, Unstably
Antonyms: Certain, Dependable, Reliable, Safe, Secure, Stable, Steady

Predominant
(Adjective)

Synonyms: Main, Chief, Important, Leading, Paramount, Prominent, Superior, Dominant, Ruling, Prevalent
Antonyms: Minor, Inferior, Unimportant, Junior, Petty, Subsidiary, Subordinate

Predicament
(Noun)

Synonyms: Plight, Puzzle, Strait, Fix, Difficulty, Jam, Perplexity
Antonyms: Assurance, Self-satisfaction, Rest, Decision, Ease, Comfort, Calmness

Prediction
(Noun)

Synonyms: Announcement, Prophecy, Forecast, Augury, Foreboding, Warning, Fortune-telling, Foresight, Divination
Antonyms: Mystery, Secrecy, Hiding, Occult, Concealment

Prejudice
(Noun)

Synonyms: Unfairness, Presumption, Preconception, Bias, Partiality

Antonyms: Certainty, Reasoning, Conviction, Demonstration, Evidence, Proof, Reason

Premature

(Adjective)

Synonyms: Rash, Unreasonable, Previous, Early, Precipitate, Untimely, Unjustified

Antonyms: Reasonable, Overdue, Late, Slow

Preserve

(Verb)

Synonyms: Care for, Conserve, Defend, Guard, Keep, Save, Secure, Shield, Continue, Retain, Sustain, Conserve, Maintain, Protect

Antonyms: Assail, Assault, Attack, Leave unprotected, Abandon, Discontinue, Drop, End, Give up, Consume, Spend, Squander, Waste

Pretend

(Verb)

Synonyms: Fabricate, Make-believe, Sham, Feign, Simulate, Profess, Allege, Counterfeit

Antonyms: Verify, Substantiate, Establish, Authentic

Prevent

(Verb)

Synonyms: Anticipate, Avert, Avoid, Balk, Bar, Block, Check, Foil, Frustrate, Hamper, Hinder, Obviate, Preclude, Restrain, Stave off, Thwart, Ward off, Stop

Antonyms: Allow, Encourage, Help, Incite, Permit, Support, Urge

Primary

(Adjective)

Synonyms: Best, Capital, Cardinal, Chief, Dominant, Elementary, First, Greatest, Highest, Leading, Main, Paramount, Prime, Principal, Top, Essential, Radical

Antonyms: Inferior, Lesser, Lowest, Subordinate,

Supplementary, Unimportant, Ensuring, Following, Later, Secondary, Subsequent, Succeeding

Privilege

(Noun)

Synonyms: Favor, Charter, Grant, Licence, Immunity, Exemption, Right, Prerogative

Antonyms: Inhibition, Veto, Prohibition, Department

Prohibit

(Verb)

Synonyms: Ban, Prevent, Preclude, Inhibit, Hinder, Disallow, Debar, Forbid, Interdict

Antonyms: Authorize, Consent to, Direct, Suffer, Tolerate, Warrant, Order, Permit, Give consent, Enjoin, Employee, Command, Allow

Prolong

(Verb)

Synonyms: Lengthen, Continue, Protract, Extend, Stretch, Sustain, Quicken, Accelerate

Antonyms: Contain, Lessen, Shorten, Diminish, Abridge, Decrease, Contract, Abbreviate, Delay

Prominent

(Adjective)

Synonyms: Conspicuous, Distinctive, Marked, Celebrated, Distinguished, Leading, Eminent, Notable, Principal

Antonyms: Inconspicuous, Minor, Union, Unimportant, Petty

Promote

(Verb)

Synonyms: Advance, Help, Push, Urge on, Raise, Further, Exhort, Assist, Excite, Elevate, Foment, Advocate, Encourage, Foster

Antonyms: Allay, Hinder, Retard, Prolong, Discourage, Divert, Degrade

Protect
(Verb)

Synonyms: Defend, Guard, Fortify, Save, Covered, Event, Guard, Harbour, Shelter, Shield

Antonyms: Expose, Betray, Assail, Assault, Expose to danger, Endanger, Threaten, Attack, Plunder

Prove
(Verb)

Synonyms: Attest, Justify, Verify, Demonstrate, Establish, Show, Confirm

Antonyms: Refuse, Negative, Deny, Refute, Disprove

Provide
(Verb)

Synonyms: Supply, Prepare, Furnish, Get, Arrange, Care, Procure, Purvey, Cater

Antonyms: Consume, Spend, Dissipate, Exhaust, Use

Prudent
(Adjective)

Synonyms: Canny, Careful, Cautions, Circumspect, Discerning, Discreet, Judicious, Politic, Sagacious, Sage, Shrewd, Vigilant, Wary

Antonyms: Careless, Heedless, Imprudent, Inconsiderate, Indiscreet, Irrational, Rash, Thoughtless, Unwise, Extravagant, Wasteful

Publish
(Verb)

Synonyms: Proclaim, Disclose, Disseminate, Advertise, Declare, Divulge, Promulgate, Broadcast, Announce.

Antonyms: Suppress, Extinguish, Smother, Repress, Conceal, Check, Cloak, Stifle, Restrain

Punish
(Verb)
Synonyms: Afflict, Chasten, Subdue, Humble, Chastise, Correct, Discipline, Castigate
Antonyms: Recompense, Indemnify, Reward, Repay, Compensate, Remunerate

Purpose
(Noun)
Synonyms: Aim, Object, Plan, Intention, End, Meaning, Resolve, Intent
Antonyms: Vague, Meaningless, Aimless, Unplanned,

Push
(Verb)
Synonyms: Press, Thrust, Shove, Jostle, Urge, Drive, Propel, Impel
Antonyms: Pull, Haul, Drag, Tow, Draw, Trail, Jerk, Deter, Tug

Put Up
(Verb)
Synonyms: Accommodate, Construct, Erect, Entertain, Present, Raise, Float, Nominate, Propose, Put forward, Recommended, Instigate, Prompt, Endure
Antonyms: Demolish, Destroy, Flatten, Knockdown, Level, Pull down, Raze, Object to, Oppose, Protest, Stand against, Reject

Q

Qualified

(Adjective)

Synonyms: Able, Accomplished, Adept, Competent, Efficient, Eligible, Equipped, Experienced, Expert, Proficient, Skillful, Talented

Antonyms: Amateur, Apprentice, Self-styled, Trainee, Uncertified, Unqualified, Untrained, Outright, Unconditional, Unequivocal

Quantity

(Noun)

Synonyms: Measure, Amount, Bulk, Number, Sum-total, Volume, Aggregate

Antonyms: Shortage, Deficiency, Insufficiency, Deficit

Quality

(Noun)

Synonyms: Status, Colouring, Gentility, Excellence, Property, Brand, Nature, Trait, Characteristic, Attribute

Antonyms: Commonness, Ordinary, Flat, Commonplace, Colorlessness

Quarrel

(Noun)

Synonyms: Wrangle, Fray, Contest, Enmity, Fight, Riot, Row, Strife, Controversy, Brawl

Antonyms: Agreement, Assent, Consent, Acquiesces, Harmony, Friendship, Peace, Amity, Equanimity, Concord

Queer

(Adjective)

Synonyms: Eccentric, Abnormal, Strange, Odd, Curious, Peculiar, Extraordinary, Unusual, Singular, Fantastic

Antonyms: Ordinary, Habitual, Everyday, Normal, Common, Usual, Commonplace

Question

(Noun)

Synonyms: Doubt, Query, Investigation, Interrogation, Inquiry, Inquisition

Antonyms: Reply, Answer, Rejoinder, Respond, Rejoin, Response

Quick

(Adjective)

Synonyms: Active, Sudden, Deft, Alive, Agile, Alert, Fast, Rapid, Swift, Perceptible

Antonyms: Listless, Slow, Inexpert, Calm, Patient, Lazy, Sluggish, Calm, Calculated

Quicken

(Verb)

Synonyms: Drive on, Hasten, Urge, Speed, Make-haste, Further, Drive, Advance, Accelerate, Expedite, Dispatch

Antonyms: Check, Obstruct, Retard, Drag, Hinder, Impede, Delay

Quiet

(Adjective)

Synonyms: Repose, Stillness, Compose, Lull, Modify, Calm, Soothe, Still, Allay, Appease, Hush, Calmness, Quietude, Rest

Antonyms : Excitement, Tumult, Commotion, Turmoil, Exasperate, Disturb, Aggravate, Disquiet, Enhance

R

Race
(Noun)

Synonyms: Tribe, Blood, Bread, Clan, Progeny, People, Family, Caste, Nation, Ethnic group
Antonyms: Unit, Individual, Humanity, Mankind, Generation, Global, Brotherhood

Racy
(Adjective)

Synonyms: Flavorful, Rich, Spicy, Spirited, Poignant, Lively
Antonyms: Cold, Vapid, Dull, Flat, State, Prosy, Insipid, Tasteless, Stupid

Radical
(Adjective)

Synonyms: Basal, Basic, Complete, Entire, Essential, Native, Extreme, Natural, Primitive, Thorough, Total, Perfect, Positive, Innate
Antonyms: Trial, Tentative, Inadequate, Conservative, Partial, Slight, Superficial

Raise
(Verb)

Synonyms: Lift, Hoist, Exalt, Increase, Collect, Grow, Breed, Cultivate, Develop, Nature, Elevate, Uplift
Antonyms: Depress, Lower, Decrease, Diminish, Lessen, Reduce, Descend

Rare

(Adjective)

Synonyms: Curious, Odd, Peculiar, Scarce, Unique, Infrequent, Remarkable, Unusual, Uncommon, Precious, Incomparable

Antonyms: Common, Usual, Frequent, Familiar, Hackneyed, Customary, Trite

Rash

(Adjective)

Synonyms: Hasty, Venturesome, Foolhardy, Indiscretions, Reckless, Precipitate, Incaution

Antonyms: Careful, Wary, Discreet, Canny, Prudent, Considered, Cautions

Rate

(Verb)

Synonyms: Appraise, Compute, Estimate, Reckon, Assess, Price

Antonyms: Miscalculate, Underrate, Undervalue

Ration

(Noun)

Synonyms: Allotment, Dole, Measure, Provision, Quota, Part, Portion, Share

Antonyms: Totality, Aggregate, Entirety, Whole, Sum total

Ready

(Adjective)

Synonyms: Quick, Speedy, Alert, Prepared, Disposed, Willing, Set

Antonyms: Unwilling, Slow, Clumsy, Unprepared,Inexperienced

Readiness

(Noun)

Have everything in readiness to have an early start.

Synonyms: Promptitude, Willingness, Eagerness, Alacrity, Quickness

Antonyms: Unwillingness, Reluctance, Disinclination, Aversion, Tardiness

Real

(Adjective)

Synonyms: Actual, Demonstrable, Genuine, True, Positive, Developed, Veritable, Essential, Certain,

Antonyms: Conceived, Reported, Visionary, Untrue, Unreal, Imaginary, Fiction, Fanciful, Illusory

Reasoning

(Adjective)

Synonyms: Rationale, Thinking, Logic, Analysis, Exposition, Generalization

Antonyms: Illogicality, Stupidity, Nonsensical, Senselessness, Foolish

Rebellion

(Noun)

Synonyms: Sedition, Insurgence, Disobedience, Heresy, Mutiny, Uprising, Insurrection, Revolt

Antonyms: Loyalty, Patriotism, Devotion, Faithfulness, Nationalism, Toadyism

Recalcitrant

(Adjective)

Synonyms: Contrary, Defiant, Insubordinate, Intractable, Obstinate, Refractory, Stubborn, Uncontrollable, Unmanageable, Unruly, Unwilling, Wayward, Willful

Antonyms: Amenable, Complaint, Docile, Obedient, Submissive

Recover

(Verb)

Synonyms: Heal, Improve, Recapture, Recoup, Redeem, Restore, Recruit, Reposes, Retrieve, Regain, Resume, Cure

Antonyms: Die, Sink, Worsen, Grow, Fail, Deteriorate, Abandon, Forfeit, Lose, Replace

Refuse

(Verb)

Synonyms: Veto, Renounce, Withhold, Decline, Exclude, Deny, Repudiate

Antonyms: Acquiesce, Agree, Grant, Cede, Admit, Accede, Assent, Allow

Release

(Verb)

Synonym : Disentangle, Exempt, Liberate, Unloose, Relieve, Free, Disengage, Extricate, Emancipate

Antonyms: Bind, Confine, Enthrall, Restrain,

Remarkable

(Adjective)

Synonyms: Extraordinary, Conspicuous, Striking, Famous, Noticeable, Strange, Distinguished

Antonyms: Ordinary, Commonplace, Customary, Normal, Average, Habitual, Medium

Reluctant

(Adjective)

Synonyms: Unwilling, Averse, Slow, Opposed, Indisposed, Backward

Antonyms: Desirous, Inclined, Willing, Eager, Disposed, Favorable

Repeal

(Verb)

Synonyms: Recall, Abolish, Revoke, Nullify, Reverse, Annul, Rescind

Antonyms: Substantiate, Ratify, Endorse, Confirm, Assent

Repentance

(Noun)

Synonyms: Contrition, Regret, Compunction, Sorrow, Penitence, Grief

Antonyms: Satisfaction, Complacence, Pleasure, Gratification

Resign
(Verb)
Synonyms: Renounce, Yield, Abandon, Quit, Leave, Surrender, Abdicate
Antonyms: Hold, Stay, Continue, Remain, Maintain, Retain, Keep

Respect
(Noun)
Synonyms: Esteem, Regard, Consideration, Accept
Antonyms: Contempt, Disregard, Disown, Ignore

Retain
(Verb)
Synonyms: Employ, Contain, Grip, Maintain, Preserve, Memories, Recall, Recollect, Engage, Maintain, Keep, Hold
Antonyms: Give up, Cede, Surrender, Relinquish, Renounce, Forsake, Abandon

Riddle
(Noun)
Synonyms: Mystery, Puzzle, Problem, Paradox, Enigma
Antonyms: Answer, Explanation, Solution, Proposition, Axiom

Risk
(Noun)
Synonyms: Hazard, Jeopardize, Venture, Peril, Danger, Imperil, Stake, Endanger
Antonyms: Security, Secure, Save, Harbor, Safety, Defend, Shelter, Shield

Rot
(Verb)
Synonyms: Decay, Corrode, Faster, Perish, Decompose, Putrefy
Antonyms: Flourish, Bloom, Expend, Flower, Increase, Grow

Rough

(Adjective)

Synonyms: Severe, Course, Irregular, Blunt, Indelicate, Hard, Tough, Difficult, Uneven

Antonyms: Calm, Regular, Delicate, Elegant, Graceful, Pleasant, Glossy, Smooth, Even, Fine, Straight

Rude

(Adjective)

Synonyms: Discourteous, Impudent, Unmannerly, Saucy, Churlish, Impertinent, Impolite

Antonyms: Civil, Cultivated, Polished, Courteous, Elegant, Genteel, Refined, Sophisticated,

S

Sacred

(Adjective)

Synonyms: Holy, Sanctified, Dedicated, Consecrated, Inviolable, Hallowed, Divine, Blessed

Antonyms: Profane, Impious, Irreverent, Irreligious, Blasphemous, Sacrilegious, Temporal, Worldly, Lay

Sad

(Adjective)

Synonyms: Woeful, Sober, Gloomy, Dull, Grave, Dejected, Depressed, Downcast, Melancholy

Antonyms: Buoyant, Merry, Glad, Gay, Joyous, Cheerful, Excited, Lively

Sanction

(Verb)

Synonyms: Allow, Support, Approve, Ratify, Endorse, Authorize, Permit, Confirm

Antonyms: Disallow, Debar, Veto, Ban, Interdict, Forbid, Prohibit

Satisfy

(Verb)

Synonyms: Glut, Appease, Assuage, Feed, Indulge, Pacify, Quench, Sate, Satiate, Meet, Slake, Surfeit, Serve, Fulfill, Suffice

Antonyms: Annoy, Displease, Dissatisfy, Exasperate, Frustrate, Give cause for complaint, Fail to meet, Dissuade, Fail to persuade

Scatter
(Verb)
Synonyms: Sprinkle, Disperse, Spread, Broadcast, Propagate, Dissipate, Distribute, Disseminate
Antonyms: Hoard, Gather, Store, Collect, Amass, Pick, Garner, Accumulate

Scanty
(Adjective)
Synonyms: Pinched, Narrow, Skimpy, Inch, Sparing, Slender, Meager, Limited, Small
Antonyms: Profuse, Abundant, Lavish, Unlimited, Sufficient, Ample, Copious, Absolute

Scold
(Verb)
Synonym: Reprimand, Castigate, Hearten, Nag, Censure, Reprove, Chide, Rebuke, Admonish
Antonyms: Compliment, Applaud, Praise, Extol, Acclaim, Approve, Commend

Seek
(Verb)
Synonyms: Hunt, Court, Inquire, Look for, Search, Solicit, Follow, Ask
Antonyms: Shun, Avoid, Eschew, Evade

Selfish
(Adjective)
Synonyms: Sordid, Greedy, Mercenary, Ungenerous, Illiberal, Mean, Selfish
Antonyms: Generous, Liberal, Charitable, Bountiful, Lavish

Sensible
(Adjective)
Synonyms: Judicious, Wise, Aware, Conscious, Observant, Intelligent, Sane, Rational, Sagacious, Cognizant

Antonyms: Unaware, Senseless, Idiotic, Stupid, Asinine, Foolish, Unconscious, Doltish

Separable

(Adjective)

Synonyms: Divisible, Classifiable, Branched, Group into

Antonyms: Indivisible, United, Inseparable

Separate

(Verb)

Synonyms: Divorce, Detach, Cleave, Remove, Sever, Estrange, Disconnect, Disengage, Disunite

Antonyms: Combine, Connect, Consolidate, Engage, Amalgamate, Joined, Unite

Settle

(Verb)

Synonyms: Conclude, Establish, Fix, Colonize, Liquidate, Finish, Domicile, Adjust, Decide, Determine

Antonyms: Ruffle, Dismantle, Confuse, Derange, Disorder

Shallow

(Adjective)

Synonyms: Trifle, Superficial, Slight, Trivial, Foolish, Unintelligent, Simple

Antonyms: Wise, Intelligent, Shrewd, Astute, Discerning, Deep, Recondite, Clever

Shame

(Noun)

Synonyms: Disgrace, Modesty, Dishonor, Shyness, Abashment, Mortification, Coyness, Abasement

Antonyms: Honor, Grace, Flare, Courage

Sharp

(Adjective)

Synonyms: Acute, Cutting, Pointed, Serrated, Abrupt, Extreme,

Alert, Apt, Astute, Bright, Clever, Discerning, Observant, Penetrating
Antonyms: Blunt, Dull, Rounded, Even, Moderate, Blurred, Dim, Slow, Stupid, Simply, Amicable, Courteous, Friendly, Bland, Mild

Shelter
(Verb)
Synonyms: Guard, Protect, Screen, Defend, Shield
Antonyms: Betray, Expel, Reject, Surrender, Refuse, Expose

Shock
(Noun)
Synonyms: Scare, Dismay, Offend, Outrage, Blow, Collision, Tremor, Disgust
Antonyms: Delight, Gladden, Please

Shoddy
(Adjective)
Synonyms: Cheap, Junky, Poor, Rubbishy, Second, Rate, Slipshod, Tacky, Tatty, Tawdry, Trashy
Antonyms: Accurate, Careful, Craftsman - like, Excellent, Fine, First - rate, Meticulous, Quality, Superlative, Well-made

Signify
(Verb)
Synonyms: Denote, Intimate, Mean, Show, Proclaim, Indicate
Antonyms: Veil, Mask, Dissemble, Cloak, Cover, Hide, Conceal

Silly
(Adjective)
Synonyms: Absurd, Senseless, Foolish, Unwise, Non-Sensual,
Antonyms: Sensible, Clever, Wise, Sapient, Intelligent

Sincere
(Adjective)
Synonyms: Genuine, True, Frank, Heart, Honest, Open,

Wholehearted
Antonyms: Affected, Untrue, Feigned, Half- hearted, Hypocritical, Insincere, Pretended

Skill

(Noun)

Synonyms: Artistry, Adroitness, Finesse, Mastery
Antonyms: Clumsiness, Incompetence, Ineptitude

Skillful

(Adjective)

Synonyms: Competent, Ingenious, Adroit, Clever, Experienced
Antonyms: Inexperienced, Bungling, Incompetent , Clumsy, Awkward

Slander

(Verb)

Synonyms: Decry, Defame, Aspersion, Opprobrious, Accuse, Malign, Disparage, Defamation
Antonyms: Praise, Eulogize, Commendation, Laud, Laudation, Commend

Slapdash

(Adjective)

Synonyms: Clumsy, Disorderly, Haphazard, Hasty, Hurried, Messy, Negligent, Perfunctory, Slipshod, Slovenly, Thoughtless, Untidy
Antonyms: Careful, Conscientious, Fastidious, Meticulous, Ordered, Orderly, Painstaking, Precise, Punctilious, Thoughtful, Tidy, Clear

Slavery

(Noun)

Synonyms: Subjugation, Thraldom, Bondage, Forced Labor, Submission, Drudgery, Servitude, Captivity
Antonyms: Freedom, Emancipation, Liberty, Independence

Slick
(Adjective)
Synonyms: Glib, Meretricious, Plausible, Polished, Smooth, Sophisticated, Adroit, Deft, Dexterous, Professional, Sharp, Skillful
Antonyms: Amateurish, Clumsy, Crude, Inexpert, Unaccomplished, Unpolished, Unprofessional

Smart
(Adjective)
Synonyms: Spruce, Trim, Elegant, Well-dressed, Immaculate, Neat, Showy
Antonyms: Rugged, Worn, Untidy, Shabby, Unkempt, Threadbare

Slow
(Adjective)
Synonyms: Gradual, Leisurely, Retarded, Slack, Sluggish
Antonyms: Agile, Fast, Quick, Rapid, Speedy, Lively

Sociable
(Adjective)
Synonyms: Companionable, Festive, Affable, Genial, Convivial
Antonyms: Secluded, Inimical, Hostile, Sequestered, Puerile, Giddy, Peevish

Soft
(Adjective)
Synonyms: Elastic, Flexible, Pliable, Pulpy, Spongy, Ductile, Yielding, Moldable, Malleable, Supple, Smooth
Antonyms: Hard, Firm, Unyielding, Compact, Rigid, Stiff

Soil
(Verb)
Synonyms: Stain, Spoil, Dirty, Smear, Pollute, Taint, Contaminate, Sully
Antonyms: Clarify, Clean, Purge, Wash, Cleanse, Purify

Solemn

(Adjective)

Synonyms: Traditional, Dignified, Grand, Grave, Majestic, Thoughtful, Ceremonial, Devotional, Pious

Antonyms: Impious, Irreligious, Sacrilegious, Irreverent

Solid

(Adjective)

Synonyms: Sound, Compact, Dense, Hard, Serious, Safe, Religious, Trustworthy, Strong

Antonyms: Unreliable, Hollow, Crumbling, Decoying, Precarious, Undependable, Unsafe

Solitary

(Adjective)

Synonyms: Unfrequented, Uninhabited, Secluded, Lonely, Isolated, Sequestered, Deserted

Antonyms: Inhabited, Popular, Well frequented, Sociable

Solve

(Verb)

Synonyms: Decipher, Decode, Unravel, Uncover

Antonyms: Baffle, Confuse, Unsolved, Puzzle

Soothe

(Verb)

Synonyms: Palliate, Alleviate, Ease, Appease, Solace, Assuage, Calm, Deaden, Tranquillize

Antonyms: Irritate, Nettle, Inflame, Agitate, Animate, Excite, Stimulate, Exasperate, Enrage

Sordid

(Adjective)

Synonyms: Dirty, Filthy, Foul, Seamy, Sleazy, Skimpy, Squalid, Wretched, Debauched, Degraded, Low, Shabby, Shameful, Vicious, Vile, Malicious, Selfish

Antonyms: Clean, Fresh, Pure, Spotless, Unblemished, Decent, Honorable, Noble, Pure, Upright

Soul

(Noun)

Synonyms: Mind, Heart, Life, Animation, Incarnation, Ardor, Ego, Essence, Vital, Principle

Antonyms: Body, Matter, Materialization, Embodiment

Spiteful

(Adjective)

Synonyms: Rancorous, Malevolent, Venomous, Vindictive, Malignant, Malicious

Antonyms: Benign, Beneficent, Benevolent, Benignant

Spread

(Verb)

Synonyms: Circulate, Expand, Escalate, Multiply, Proclaim, Publish, Development, Escalation, Distribute, Propagate

Antonyms: Accumulate, Contain, Control, Curb, Repress, Restrain, Gather

Splendid

(Adjective)

Synonyms: Resplendent, Magnificent, Grand, Impressive, Luxurious, Superb, Radiant, Brilliant, Beaming, Shining

Antonyms: Dull, Dark, Dim, Tarnished, Depressing, Disgusting, Mediocre, Pathetic, Sordid, Cloudy

Statement

(Noun)

Synonyms: Account, Narration, Declaration, Avowal, Assertion, Announcement, Utterance

Antonyms: Refutation, Disavowal, Contradiction, Denial, Negation

Spontaneous
(Adjective)
Synonyms: Extempore, Free, Impromptu, Impulsive, Instinctive, Natural, Unbidden, Uncompelled, Unforced, Unprompted, Voluntary, Willing
Antonyms: Arranged, Calculated, Contrived, Deliberate, Forced, Mannered, Orchestrated, Planned, Premeditated, Preplanned

Steady
(Adjective)
Synonyms: Constant, Undeviating, Stable, Regular, Firm, Consistent, Uniform
Antonyms: Irregular, Unstable, Wavering, Changeable, Variable, Unsteady, Inconsistent

Steep
(Adjective)
Synonyms: High, Headlong, Sheer, Exorbitant, Sharp, Abrupt, Precipitous
Antonyms: Gradual, Low level, Straight, Easy, Gentle

Stiff
(Adjective)
Synonyms: Brittle, Firm, Hard, Rigid, Solid, Taunt, Tense, Tight, Clumsy, Crude, Arduous, Formidable, Tough, Cruel, Drastic, Extreme, Strong
Antonyms: Ductile, Elastic, Flexible, Pliable, Plaint, Limber, Supple, Casual, Easy, Informal, Natural, Relaxed, Spontaneous

Still
(Adjective)
Synonyms: Motionless, Calm, Peaceful, Serene, Stagnant, Quiet, Stationary, Pacific
Antonyms: Moving, Flowing, Excited, Disturbed, Troubled, Agitated, Running, Flustered

Stimulate
(Verb)
Synonyms: Instigate, Whet, Purr, Inflame, Inspirit, Good, Provoked, Incite, Motivate
Antonyms: Prevent, Hinder, Deter, Dissuade

Stimulus
(Noun)
Synonyms: Spur, Incitement, Inducement, Incentive
Antonyms: Deterrent, Dissuasion, Hindrance

Strange
(Adjective)
Synonyms: Queer, Extraordinary, Unique, Unnatural, Unusual, Uncommon, Odd, Eccentric, Inexplicable
Antonyms: Normal, Common, Familiar, Habitual, Standard, Everyday, Usual, Natural, Ordinary

Stop
(Verb)
Synonyms: Block, Arrest, Cease, Halt, Prevent, Discontinue
Antonyms: Begin, Activate, Continue, Quicken, Purr

Strong
(Adjective)
Synonyms: Muscular, Fit, Healthy, Robust, Stalwart, Shout, Sturdy, Reinforced, Athletic, Powerful, Tough
Antonyms: Powerless, Delicate, Feeble, Faint, Mild, Timid, Pale, Weak, Soft

Sublime
(Adjective)
Synonyms: Superb, Grand, Lofty, Majestic, Noble, Glorious, Exalted, Splendid, Resplendent, Beautiful
Antonyms: Powerless, Lowly, Mundane, Ordinary, Poor, Ridiculous, Bad, Common place, Mean, Insignificant, Weak, Soft

Submissive

(Adjective)

Synonyms: Abject, Accommodating, Acquiescent, Amenable, Complaint, Deferential, Docile, Dutiful, Humble, Obedient, Passive, Plaint, Tractable, Unresisting

Antonyms: Awkward, Difficult, Disobedient, Head strong, Intractable, Obstinate, Stubborn, Uncooperative, Unyielding

Substantial

(Adjective)

Synonyms: Actual, Material, Tangible, Palpable, Perceptible, Corporeal, Real, Existing

Antonyms: Illusive, Unsubstantial, Illusory, Unreal, Chimerical, Shadowy, Fanciful, Farcical

Stubborn

(Adjective)

Synonyms: Adamant, Fixed, Bull – headed, Obdurate, Tenacious, Unhanding

Antonyms: Adaptable, Complaint, Irresolute, Malleable, Pliable, Vacating, Pliable, Headstrong, Inflexible, Obstinate, Docile, Flexible

Stupid

(Adjective)

Synonyms: Dense, Dull, Slow, Thick, Unintelligent

Antonyms: Bright, Clever, Intelligent, Keen, Smart

Suitable

(Adjective)

Synonyms: Appropriate, Eligible, Pertinent, Relevant, Fitting, Seemly, Convenient, Becoming

Antonyms: Unsuitable, Inappropriate, Irrelevant, Unseemly, Untimely, Improper

Sudden

(Adjective)

Synonyms: Momentary, Brief, Rapid, Quick, Unexpected, Rash, Unanticipated, Unforeseen

Antonyms: Awaited, Gradual, Anticipated, Progressive

Summon

(Verb)

Synonyms: Call, Bid, Arouse, Assemble, Convene, Invite, Rouse, Convoke, Invoke, Send for

Antonyms: Dismiss, Postpone, Adjourn

Superb

(Adjective)

Synonyms: Admirable, Breathtaking, Brill, Choice, Divine, Excellent, Exquisite, Five, Gorgeous, Grand, Magnificent, Marvelous, Superior, Superlative

Antonyms: Abysmal, Awful, Bad, Disappointing, Dreadful, Inferior, Mediocre, Pathetic, Poor quality, Run-of-mill, Terrible, Woeful

Superficial

(Adjective)

Synonyms: External, Shallow, Slight, Outward, Hasty, Casual, Cursory, Empty, Frivolous, Lightweight, Silly

Antonyms: Penetrating, Deep, Thorough, Profound, Detailed, Serious, Comprehensive

Sure

(Adjective)

Synonyms: Certain, Assured, Clear, Confident, Accurate, Trustworthy, Persuaded, Positive, Satisfied, Definite, Doubtless, Positive

Antonyms: Doubtful, Uncertain, Unsure, Wavering, Improbable, Vague, Unreliable, Insecure

Surprising
(Adjective)

Synonyms: Unexpected, Marvelous, Startling, Striking, Astonishing, Amazing, Suddenness

Antonyms: Everyday, Ordinary, Usual, Normal, Customary, Habitual

Suppress
(Verb)

Synonyms: Subdue, Overpower, Bridle, Quash, Restrain, Quell, Check, Moderate, Repress, Impede

Antonyms: Inflame, Encourage, Incite, Promote, Stimulate, Spread, Gee up, Excite, Provoke, Agitate, Kindle

Suspend
(Verb)

Synonyms: Debar, Stay, Hinder, Stop, Withhold, Interrupt, Discontinue, Fall, Defer, Delay

Antonyms: Begin, Keep up, Urge on, Protract, Continue, Expedite, Prolong

Surrender
(Verb)

Synonyms: Leave, Resign, Yield, Waive, Let so, Leave, Give up, Over, Code, Alienate, Abandon

Antonyms: Withhold, Hold, Defy, Oppose, Resist, Withstand, Reserve, Retain, Detain

Swell
(Verb)

Synonyms: Distend, Enlarge, Extend, Increase, Rise, Bulge, Bloat, Billow, Belly, Magnify, Bungle, Amplify, Dilate, Enhance, Expand

Antonyms: Shorten, Contract, Reduce, Decrease, Diminish, Abridge, Attenuate

Sympathy
(Noun)

Synonyms: Accord, Kindness, Pity, Condolence, Commiseration, Tenderness, Harmony, Rapport, Warmth, Love, Fellow-feeling, Compassion

Antonyms: Pitilessness, Cruelty, Hard – heartedness, Selfishness

Systematic
(Adjective)

Synonyms: Methodical, Efficient, Organized, Precise, Standardized, Regular, Orderly

Antonyms: Irregular, Casual, Fortuitous, Unmethodical, Occasional

T

Taciturn

(Adjective)

Synonyms: Mute, Quiet, Reserved, Reticent, Silent, Tight – lipped, Unforth coming, Withdrawn

Antonyms: Chatty, Communicative, Forth coming, Garrulous, Loquacious, Open, Outgoing, Sociable, Talkative, Verbose, Voluble, Wordy

Tact

(Noun)

Synonyms: Finesse, Diplomacy, Adroitness, Finesse, Discretion, Skill, Cleverness, Consideration

Antonyms: Discourtesy, Frankness, Awkward, Clumsy, Gauche, Untoward, Roughness, Bluntness, Simplicity

Talent

(Noun)

Synonyms: Ability, Capacity, Flair, Endowment, Power, Knack, Genius, Aptitude, Skill

Antonyms: Inefficiency, Unskillfulness, Idleness, Stupidity

Tasty

(Adjective)

Synonyms: Appetizing, Luscious, Delicious, Palatable

Antonyms: Nasty, Sickening, Nauseous, Flavorless, Insipid

Teacher

(Noun)

Synonyms: Professor, Instructor, Lecturer, Preceptor,

Schoolmaster, Master
Antonyms: Student, Pupil, Disciple, Learner

Teaching
(Noun)
Synonyms: Instruction, Education, Tutorship, direction, Guidance, Practice, Indoctrination, Exercise
Antonyms: Learn, Go to school, Acquire, Skill, Be instructed, Read

Tear
(Verb)
Synonyms : Rip, Rend, Shred, Sunder, Dust, Dash, Speed, Seize, Snatch, Pluck, Split, Lacerate, Sever, Rupture, Division
Antonyms: Repair, Patch, Rectify, Restore, Mend

Tease
(Verb)
Synonyms: Irritate, Chafe, Provoke, Bait, Goad, Pester, Taunt, Vex, Plague, Torment, Annoy,
Antonyms: Hush, Compose, Conciliate, Appease, Calm, Mollify

Tedious
(Adjective)
Synonyms: Banal, Drab, Dreary, Dull, Irksome, Laborious, Monotonous, Prosaic, Soporific, Tiresome, Tiring, Vapid, Wearisome
Antonyms: Enjoyable, Enthralling, Exciting, Exhilarating, Imaginative, Inspiring, Interesting, Quickly, Finished, Short, Stimulating

Temperamental
(Adjective)
Synonyms: Capricious, Easily, Upset, Emotional, Erratic, Excitable, Fiery, Highly strong, Hypersensitive, Impatient, Irritable, Moody, Neurotic, Passionate, Petulant, Sensitive

Antonyms: Calm, Cool headed, Easy going, Phlegmatic, Unexcitable, Constant, Dependable, Reliable, Stable, Steady

Tempt

(Verb)

Synonyms: Reduce, Decoy, Inveigle, Entice, Contrive, Wheedle, Coax, Invite, Lure, Attract, Allure

Antonyms: Deter, Disincline, Discourage, Care, Restraint, Dissuade

Temporary

(Adjective)

Synonyms: Fleeting, Evanescent, Passing, Ephemeral, Momentary, Transitory, Transient

Antonyms: Everlasting, Immortal, Invariable, Permanent, Persistent

Tendency

(Noun)

Synonyms: Prone, Inclination, Predilection, Leaning, Penchant, Trend, Bias, Proclivity, Propensity

Antonyms: Aversion, Distaste, Dislike, Disinclination, Antipathy, Detestation

Terse

(Adjective)

Synonyms: Neat, Short, Succinct, Laconic, Compact, Summary, Sententious, Condensed

Antonyms: Diffuse, Circumlocutory, Confused, Discursive, Rambling, Verbose, Lengthy, Wordy

Theory

(Noun)

Synonyms: Belief, Postulate, Assumption, Speculation, Doctrine, Conjecture, Hypothesis, Supposition

Antonyms: Practical, Realistic, Actual, Happening

Thick
(Adjective)
Synonyms: Broad, Bulky, Deep, Solid, Substantial, Close, Clotted, Opaque, Abundant, Brimming, Bristling, Covered, Crawling, Replete
Antonyms: Narrow, Slight, Slim, Thin, Clear, Diluted, Runny, Weak, Bare, Empty, Free from, Sparse, Distant

Thin
(Adjective)
Synonyms: Diluted, Narrow, Slim, Bony, Lean, Slender, Delicate, Weak, Meager, Films, Scanty, Sparse
Antonyms: Strong, Sturdy, Heavy, Thick, Bulky, Adequate, Plentiful, Abundant, Profuse, Bountiful, Wholesome

Thoughtful
(Adjective)
Synonyms: Attentive, Circumspect, Heedful, Provident, Careful, Considerate, Mindful
Antonyms: Carefree, Gay, Remiss, Reckless, Negligent, Neglectful, Giddy

Timely
(Adjective)
Synonyms: Appropriate, Convenient, Punctual, Prompt, Early, Seasonable, Opportune
Antonyms: Tardy, Unseasonable, Late, Inopportune

Timid
(Adjective)
Synonyms: Bashful, Afraid, Coward, Coy, Nervous, Diffident, Shy, Chicken-hearted, Timorous, Submissive
Antonyms: Audacious, Brace, Daring, Confident, Poised, Aggressive, Arrogance, Fearless, Shameless

Tired
(Adjective)
Synonyms: Drained, Drowsy, Enervated, Fatigued, Flagging,

Sleepy, Weary, Exasperated, Irked, Irritated, Exhausted, Weary, Worn-out
Antonyms: Invigorated, Refreshed, Rested, Relaxed, Strengthened

Toleration

(Noun)

Synonyms: Tolerance, Temperance, Endurance, Laxity, Forgiveness, Clemency, Moderation
Antonyms: Irritation, Heating up, Wearing off, Rigidity, Overbearance, Dogmatism, Fanaticism

Torture

(Noun)

Synonyms: Anguish, Afflict, Crucify, Pain, Persecute, Pain, Agony, Torment, Distress, Persecute
Antonyms: Allay, Soothe, Alleviate, Console, Solace, Mollify, Relief, Comfort, Palate, Ease, Deaden, Lessen

Touchy

(Adjective)

Synonyms: Bad tempered, Captious, Cross, Grumpy, Irascible, Irritable, Peevish, Petulant, Querulous, Oversensitive, Surly
Antonyms: Affable, Cheerful, Easy-going, Genial, Imperious, Indifferent, Insensitive, Pleasant, Sunny, Sweet, Unconcerned

Tragedy

(Noun)

Synonyms: Misfortune, Disaster, Affliction, Adversity, Calamity, Catastrophe
Antonyms: Farce, Happiness, Joy, Prosperity, Success, Comedy, Humor, Drama

Transparent

(Adjective)

Synonyms: Clear, Lucid, Obvious, Apparent, Distinct, Limpid, Crystalline

Antonyms: Foggy, Obscure, Cloudy, Muddy, Opaque, Thick, Hidden, Vague, Uncertain

Treacherous
(Adjective)

Synonyms: Disloyal, Deceitful, Duplicitous, Faithlessness, False, Perfidious, Unreliable, Untrue, Unfaithful, Unreliable, Not trustworthy, Perfidious

Antonyms: Faithful, Loyal, Trustee, Devoted, Reliable, Trustworthy

Transient
(Adjective)

Synonyms: Brief, Fleeting, Fugitive, Short, Transitory, Livid, Momentary, Flying, Passing, Evanescent, Temporary, Ephemeral

Antonyms: Long lasting, Detailed, Permanent, Persistent

Tremble
(Verb)

Synonyms: Vibrate, Shake, Quake, Shiver, Shudder, Tester, Totter, Shudder, Oscillate, Quiver

Antonyms: Stiffen, Petrify, Steady

Trick
(Noun)

Synonyms: Wiles, Deception, Dodge, Fraud, Swindle, Play, Skill, Ruse, Guile, Imposture, Cunning

Antonyms: Innocence, Frankness, Guilelessness, Truth, Sincerity

Trust
(Noun)

Synonyms: Reliance, Confidence, Keeping, Credit, Office, Duty, Expectation, Hope, Credence, Belief

Antonyms: Distrust, Faithlessness, Breaking of pledge, Deception

Try
(Verb)

Synonyms: Essay, Strive, Effort, Seek, Struggle, Undertake, Endeavour, Attempt

Antonyms: Leave, Drop, Quit, Give up, Relinquish, Abandon

Tyranny
(Noun)

Synonyms: Totalitarianism, Autocracy, Oppression, Despotism, Rigor, Harshness

Antonyms: Pity , Love, Compassion, Softness, Sympathy

Topical
(Adjective)

Synonyms: Indicative, Symbolical, Regular, Illustrative, Normal

Antonyms: Abnormal, Singular, Divergent, Peculiar

U

Ugly

(Adjective)

Synonyms: Homely, Distasteful, Frightful, Hideous, Repugnant, Terrible, Baleful, Menacing, Evil, Dark, Nasty, Spiteful, Sullen, Plain, Unattractive, Unsightly

Antonyms: attractive, Beautiful, Cute, Gorgeous, Handsome, Lovely, Pretty, Pleasant, Agreeable, Charming

Unalterable

Synonyms: Variable, Immutable, Changeless, Unchangeable, Permanent, Constant

Antonyms: Revocable, Mutable, Changeable, Variable, Inconstant, Alterable

Unanimity

(Noun)

Synonyms: Harmony, Assent, Concert, Concurrence, Unity, Unison, Like-mindedness, Agreement, Accord, Concord

Antonyms: Disagreement, Contention, Difference, Variance, Disharmony

Unanimous

Synonyms: Agreeing, Concordant, United

Antonyms: Disagreeing, Differing, Discordant, Deviating

Unanswerable

Synonyms: Conclusive, Incontrovertible, Certain, Infallible, Irrefutable, Undeniable

Antonyms: Refutable, Inconclusive, Disputable, Fallible, Weak

Uncertain

(Adjective)

Synonyms: Fluctuating, Unreliable, Changeable, Precarious, Inconstant, Fitful, Irregular

Antonyms: Trustworthy, Unchangeable, Reliable, Stable, Regular, Steady

Unconcerned

(Adjective)

Synonyms: Cool, Disinterested, Indifferent, Nonchalant, Easy, Apathetic

Antonyms: Solicitous, Interested, Concerned, Anxious

Unconquerable

(Adjective)

Synonyms: Insuperable, Invincible, Indomitable, Insurmountable

Antonyms: Weak, Powerless, Feeble, Conquerable

Under

(Preposition & Adjective)

Synonyms: Inferior, Below, Underneath, Lower, Subordinate, Beneath

Antonyms: Overhead, Above, Over

Understand

(Verb)

Synonyms: Apprehend, Discern, Comprehend, Realise, Perceive, Grasp

Antonyms: Misunderstand, Misinterpret, Misconceive

Undertake

(Verb)

Synonyms: Engage, Stipulate, Guarantee, Promise, Agree

Antonyms: Unconditional, Free, Independent

Undertaking

(Noun)

Synonyms: Contract, Endeavor, Trade, Enterprise, Promise, Engagement, Venture

Antonyms: Irresponsibility, Refusal, Truancy, Escapade, Avoidance

Unfair

(Adjective)

Synonyms: Biased, Unjust, Bigoted, Discriminatory, Unethical, Inequitable, Partial, Dishonest, Wrongful

Antonyms: Fair, Just, Honest, Unprejudiced, Natural, Impartial, Equitable

Unfaithful

(Verb)

Synonyms: Unreliable, Treacherous, Inconstant

Antonyms: Trustworthy, Loyal, Faithful, Staunch, Reliable

Unfit

(Verb)

Synonyms: Unqualified, Inapt, Inappropriate, Incapable, Improper, Unsuitable

Antonyms: Suitable, Pertinent, Relevant, Proper, Fit, Appropriate

Unfortunate

(Verb)

Synonyms: Deplorable, Infelicitous, Frustrated, Luckless, Calamitous, Unlucky

Antonyms: Auspicious, Lucky, Favourable, Happy, Fortunate

Unhappiness

(Noun)

Synonyms: Wrcchedness, Distress, Sorrow, Woe, Misery

Antonyms: Happiness, Gaiety, Blessedness, Cheerfulness

Unhappy

(Adjective)

Synonyms: Unlucky, Unfortunate, Calamitous, Disastrous
Antonyms: Favourable, Fortunate, Lucky

Unholy

(Adjective)

Synonyms: Profane, Unrighteous, Depraved, Wicked, Sinful, Irreligious
Antonyms: Holy, Divine, Religious, Morel

Union

(Noun)

Synonyms: Unity, Juncture, Junction, Coalition, Concert, Cooperation, Combination, Unification, Oneness
Antonyms: Analysis, Contrairity, Disassociation, Separation, Divorce, Division, Disconnection, Schism

Unite

(Verb)

Synonyms: Combine, Amalgamate, Link, Meld, Join, Knit, Merge, Ally, Associate, Collaborate, Pool, Coalesce, Blend
Antonyms: Scatter, Detach, Disunite, Disjoin, Break, Divide, Part, Separate, Unconnected

Universal

(Adjective)

Synonyms: All embracing, International, Complete, General, Whole, Comprehensive, Entire
Antonyms: Parochial, Sectarian, Partisan, Sectional, Factional

Unusual

(Adjective)

Synonyms: Extraordinary, Remarkable, Peculiar, Uncommon, Exceptional, Rare, Singular
Antonyms: Usual, Common, Hackneyed, Habitual, Commonplace

Uphold

(Verb)

Synonyms: Champion, Back, Support, Maintain, Defend, Sustain

Antonyms: Betray, Drop, Destroy, Demolish, Destruct

Upset

(Verb)

Synonyms: Disturb, Disorder, Spoil, Agitate, Dismay, Grieve, Perturb, Trouble, Disconcert, Disrupt

Antonyms: Soothe, Calm, Relieve, Relax

Urgent

(Adjective)

Synonyms: Critical, Pressing, Important, Insistent, Imperative

Antonyms: Minor, Inconsiderable, Unimportant, Trifling, Insignificant, Petty, Trivial

Usual

(Adjective)

Synonyms: Common, Accustomed, Customary, Familiar, Regular, Ordinary, Regular

Antonyms: Occasional, Specific, Unusual, Exceptional, Peculiar, Unparalled

Utility

(Noun)

Synonyms: Service, Use, Advantage, Profit, Policy, Benefit, Avail, Usefulness, Serviceableness

Antonyms: Disadvantages, Worthless, Useless

V

Vacant

(Adjective)

Synonyms: Devoid, Unemployed, Untenanted, Unoccupied, Waste, Vacuous, Unfilled, Leisure, Blank, Empty

Antonyms: Occupied, Replete, Packed, Filled, Full, Brimful, Brimming, Jammed, Busy, Crammed, Gorged

Vague

(Adjective)

Synonyms: Haze, Dim, Obscure, Indistinct, Indefinite

Antonyms: Clear, Defined, Plain, Definite, Exact, Lucid, Well-defined, Sensible

Valid

(Adjective)

Synonyms: Binding, Defensible, Powerful, Efficacious, Cogent, Logical

Antonyms: Invalid, Unconvincing, Unsound, Lame, Feeble, Weak, Illogical

Valuable

(Adjective)

Synonyms: Expensive, precious, costly

Antonyms: Worthless, cheap, valueless, base

Value

(Noun)

Synonyms: Appraise, Assess, Estimate

Antonyms: Un-estimated, Priceless

Vanish

(Verb Intransitive)

Synonyms: Dissolve, Disappear, Depart, Suddenly fade away
Antonyms: Appear, Arrive, Emerge

Vanity

(Noun)

Synonyms: Arrogance, Conceit, Pride, Egotism
Antonyms: Unobtrusiveness, Modesty, Meekness

Variety

(Noun)

Synonyms: Many-sidedness, Assortment, Variation, Difference
Antonyms: Recurrence, Sameness, Repetitiveness, Dullness

Various

(Adjective)

Synonyms: Different, Multitudinous, Numerous, Variegated, Sundry, Manifold, Many, Several, Multiform
Antonyms: Identical, Alike, Same, Similar, Uniform, Few, Exceptional

Vehement

(Adjective)

Synonyms: Ardent, Emphatic, Fervent, Forceful, Eager, Earnest, Passionate
Antonyms: Feeble, Mild, Affected, Cool, Moderate, Apathetic, Calm

Verbal

(Adjective)

Synonyms: Spoken, oral, unwritten
Antonyms: Inscribed, printed, recorded, written

Versatile

Synonyms: Mercurial, Constant, Volatile, Capricious, Unsteady, Changeable

Antonyms: Invariable, Unchangeable, Undeviating, Steady, Constant, Unwavering, Permanent

Vertical

Synonyms: Erect, Perpendicular, Upright
Antonyms: Oblique, Slanting, Horizontal, Inclining, Sloping

Very

(Adjective)

Synonyms: Extremely, Exceptionally, Exceedingly, Highly, Excessively
Antonyms: Sameness, Lowly, Smooth

Vibrate

(Verb)

Synonyms: Swing, Sway, Quiver, Shiver
Antonyms: Congeal, Gell, Solidify

Victory

(Noun)

Synonyms: Success, Achievement, Mastery, Conquest, Triumph, Supremacy
Antonyms: Defeat, Frustration, Descent, Fall, Subservience, Failure

View

(Noun)

Synonyms: Watch, Behold, Contemplate, Inspect, Eye, Scan, See
Antonyms: Ignore, Neglect, Disgregard

Vigilant

(Adjective)

Synonyms: Alert, Wakeful, Cautious, On the look out, Wary, Wide-awake, Watchful, Circumspect
Antonyms: Careless, Uncautious, Inconsiderable, Negligent, Neglectful, Unwary, Heedless, Inattentive

Violation
(Noun)
Synonyms: Trespass, Breach, Encroachment, Sacrilege, Infraction, Infringement, Transgression
Antonyms: Compliance, Observance, Acquiescence, Adherence, Concurrence

Violent
(Adjective)
Synonyms: Wild, Sharp, Server, Acute, Turbulent, Infuriate, Immoderate, Impetuous, Fierce, Frantic, Intense, Mad, Raging, Raving, Tumultous
Antonyms: Frigid, Peaceful, Unruffled, Quiet, Cool, Collected, Placid

Virtue
(Noun)
Synonyms: Chastity, Truth, Uprightness, Rectitude, Faithfulness, Duty, Worth, Worthiness, Rightness, Justice, Honour, Honestly
Antonyms: Wrong, Depravity, Viciousness, Wickedness, Evil, Vice, Failing, Corruption

Vision
(Noun)
Synonyms: Sight, Seeing
Antonyms: Blindness, Sightlessness

Visitor
Synonyms: Caller, Guest, Company
Antonyms: Host

Vital
(Adjective)
Synonyms: Alive, Indispensable, Necessary, Animate, Living, Important, Essential
Antonyms: Immaterial, Inert, Unimportant, Insignificant, Dead, Trifling, Lifeless,

Vivid

(Adjective)

Synonyms: Bright, Telling, Graphic, Brilliant, Glaring, Expressive

Antonyms: Dim, Dull, Tarnished

Voice

(Noun)

Synonyms: Talk, Speaking, Utterance, Address

Antonyms: Speechlessness, Stillness, Hush, Silence

Void

(Adjective)

Synonyms: Abolish, Repeal, Revoke, Negate, Nullify, Cancel

Antonyms: Endorse, Legalize, Establish, Permit, Renew, Uphold

Voluntary

(Adjective)

Synonyms: Gratuitous, Discretional, Intentional, Spontaneous, Willing, Unconstrained, Optional, Automatic, Instinctive

Antonyms: Enforced, Imperative, Compulsory, Automatic, Instinctive, Obligatory

Vulgar

(Adjective)

Synonyms: Coarse, Crude, Dirty, Impolite, Indecent, Rude, Nasty, Gaudy, Gross, Obscene

Antonyms: Exquisite, Polite, Aristocratic, Elegant, Genteel, Refined, Polished

W

Wages

(Noun)

Synonyms: Compensation, Remuneration, Payment, Hire, Salary, Reward

Antonyms: Unproductivity, Fruitless, Rewardless, Waste

Wait

(Verb)

Synonyms: Await, Remain, Half, Stop

Antonyms: Press, Move, Urge

Wakeful

(Adjective)

Synonyms: Active, Vigilant, Awake, Watchful

Antonyms: Asleep, Inactive, Quiescent, Lethargic, Sleeping, Slumbering

Walk

(Verb)

Synonyms: Stroll, Saunter, Hike, Tramp, Ramble

Antonyms: Hasten, Run, Hurry, Race, Sprint

Wander

(Verb)

Synonyms: Ramble, Range, Deviate, Depart, Roam, Digress

Antonyms: Abide, Rest, Settle

Wane

(Verb)

Synonyms: Abate, Atrophy, Decrease, Diminish, Drop, Dwindle, Fail, Lesson

Antonyms: Blossom, Brighten, Develop, Expand, Grow, Improve, Increase, Rise, Strengthen, Wax

Want

(Noun)

Synonyms: Indigence, Penury, Poverty, Privation

Antonyms: Affluence, Plenty, Prosperity, Wealth

War

(Noun)

Synonyms: Contention, Discord, Battle, Hostility, Strife

Antonyms: Peace, Calm, Harmony, Concord, Agreement

Wash

(Verb)

Synonyms: Lave, Clean, Cleanse, Rinse

Antonyms: Soil, Pollute, Dirty, Contaminate, Besmirch, Defile, Begrime

Washing

Synonyms: Ablution, Bathing, Cleansing, Purification, Lavation, Cleaning, Bath.

Antonyms: Taint, Staining Stain, Contamination, Pollution, Defiling, Defilement, Soiling, Soil, Befouling.

Wasteful

(Adjective)

Synonyms: Prodigal, Spendthrift, Lavish, Improvident, Imprudent, Unthrifty, Reckless

Antonyms: Sparing, Miserly, Economical, Prudent, Frugal, Provident, Thrifty

Wavering
(Adjective)

Synonyms: Oscillating, Unsteady, Fluctuating, Undecided, Undetermined, Inconstant, Vacillating, Faltering, Quivering
Antonyms: Steady, Unwavering, Determined, Firm, Resolute, Unhesitating, Steadfast

Weak
(Adjective)

Synonyms: Decrepit, Feeble, Delicate, Effete, Faint, Enervated, Frail, Inform
Antonyms: Energetic, Hardy, Healthy, Strong, Stout, Sturdy, Tough

Weaken
(Verb)

Synonyms: Attenuate, Enfeeble, Sap, Impair, Debilitate, Universe
Antonyms: Strengthen, Fortify, Brace, Boost, Enhance, Improve, Invigorate, Harden, Create

Weakness
(Noun)

Synonyms: Lassitude, Debility, Languor, Infirmity, Frailty
Antonyms: Strength, Might, Energy, Vigour

Wealth
(Noun)

Synonyms: Abundance, Substance, Riches, Profusion, Money, Pelf, Plenty, Prosperity, Property, Possessions
Antonyms: Poverty, Destitution, Privations, Distress, Want, Impecunity, Insufficiency

Wedding
(Noun)

Synonyms: Wedlock, Marriage, Nuptial
Antonyms: Divorce, Separation

Weight
(Noun)

Synonyms: Gravity, Moment, Importance, Consequence, Significance
Antonyms: Triviality, Insignificance, Unimportance

Welcome
(Transitive Verb)

Synonyms: Reception, Salutation, Meeting, Greeting, Cordial, Handshake
Antonyms: Adieu, Goodbye, Leave-taking, Parting, Departure, Godspeed

Wet
(Adjective)

Synonyms: Damp, Humid, Rainy, Drenched, Showery, Moist, Soak
Antonyms: Parch, Parched, Dry, Arid, Dehydrate

Whiten

Synonyms: Bleach, Blanch, Etiolate
Antonyms: Darken, Smudge, Blacken

Wholly

Synonyms: Absolutely, Perfectly, Entirely, Utterly, Completely, Totally, Fully
Antonyms: Incompletely, Partly, Partially

Wicked
(Adjective)

Synonyms: Iniquitous, Criminal, Vile, Villainous, Corrupt, Evil, Immoral, Bad, Heinous, Sinful
Antonyms: Virtuous, Benevolent, Ethical, Honorable, Noble, Incorrupt, Chaste, Moral, Upright

Wide
(Adjective)

Synonyms: Expansive, Spacious, Large, Broad, Extensive

Antonyms: Narrow, Cramped, Confined, Circumscribed, Close, Limited, Small

Wild

(Adjective)

Synonyms: Ferocious, Fierce, Uncivilized, Barbarous, Rude violent, Furious, Savage

Antonyms: Gentle, Timid, Harmless, Domesticated

Will

(Verb)

Synonyms: Wish, Resolution, Decision, Volition, Desire, Determination, Inclination

Antonyms: Neutral, Indifferent, Impartial, Unwillingness

Willingly

(Adjective)

Synonyms: Voluntarily, Gladly, With pleasure, Freely, Readily

Antonyms: Unwillingly, Reluctantly

Win

Synonyms: Persuade, Procure, Gain, Acquire, Attain, Obtain, Influence, Away, Get, Achieve

Antonyms: Lose, Fail

Winding

Synonyms: Twisting, Curving, Sinuous, Meandering, Tortuous, Serpentine, Bending

Antonyms: Direct, Straight, Underviating

Wisdom

(Noun)

Synonyms: Intelligence, Discretion, Sense, Learning, Erudition, Discernment, Knowledge, Sagacity, Prudence

Antonyms: Stupidity, Absurdity, Idiocy, Nonsense, Ignorance, Silly

Wise
(Noun)
Synonyms: Prudent, Judicious, Intelligent, Sensible, Discreet, Sapient, Sagacious
Antonyms: Senseless, Dull, Stupid, Silly, Indiscreet, Irrational, Absurd

Wonder
(Noun)
Synonyms: Wonderment, Bewilder, Amazedness, Miraculousness, Marvel, Amazement, Sensation, Electrification
Antonyms: Principle, Castle in the air, Expectation, Theory, Result

Wood
(Noun)
Synonyms: Jungle, Thicket, Grove, Woodland, Copse,
Antonyms: City, Town

Word
(Noun)
Synonyms: Pledge, Promise, Assurance, Expression, Term
Antonyms: Idea, Thought, Supposition

Work
(Noun)
Synonyms: Grind, Product, Deed, Action, Employment, Labour, Drudgery, Exertion, Business
Antonyms: Leisure, Recreation, Relaxation, Repose, Idleness, Ease

Workman
(Noun)
Synonyms: Mechanic, Employee, Labourer, Toiler, Craftsman
Antonyms: Controller, Superintendent, Manager, Master

Worthless

(Noun)

Synonyms: Degraded, Valueless, Dissolute, Cheap, Base, Despicable, Paltry, Contemptible

Antonyms: Transcendent, Estimable, Excellent, Good, Costly, Valuable, Admirable

X

Xanthic

(Adjective)

Synonyms: Light–skinned, Golden–haired, Yellow–haired, Fair – haired, Blonde, Fair

Antonyms: Brown, Black, Wheatish, Skinned

Y

Yawn

(Verb)

Synonyms: Gape, Open, Wide, Part, Split
Antonyms: Close, Shut, Abridge, Shorten, Peephole

Yearn

(Verb Intransitive)

Synonyms: Hanker, Long, Wish, Desire
Antonyms: Hope for, Secure, Get, Expect

Yeoman

Synonyms: Petty officer, Beef-eater, Commander, Retainer
Antonyms: Officer, Landlord, Lord, Governor, Boss

Yield

(Verb)

Synonyms: Give–way, Submit, Accede, Waive, Surrender, Renounce, Abandon, Forgo, Crop, Harvest
Antonyms: Resist, Withstand, Refuse, Keep back, Withhold, Restrain, Oppose, Assail, Contend, Confront

Yoke

(Noun)

Synonyms: Link , Connect, Harness, Couple, String
Antonyms: Release, Divorce, Abandon, Disconnect

Young

(Adjective)

Synonyms: Youthful, Boyish, New, Fresh, Childish, Recent

Antonyms: Mature, Elderly, Aged, Ripe, Late, Full,

Yell

(Verb)

Synonyms: Scream, Screech, Howl, Shrink, Cry, Bawl
Antonyms: Mumble, Mutter, Murmur, Whisper

Z

Zeal
(Noun)
Synonyms: Zest, Dedication, Eagerness, Devotion, Earnestness, Warmth, Energy
Antonyms: Coolness, Weakness, Laziness, Carelessness, Apathy

Zenith
(Noun)
Synonyms: Acme, Apex, Climax, Crest, Peak, Pinnacle, Summit, Top, Apogee
Antonyms: Base, Bottom, Depths, Lowest point, Nadir, Rock bottom

Zest
(Noun)
Synonyms: Enjoyment, Gusto, Relish, Charm, Pungency, Taste, Delectation
Antonyms: Abhorrence, Apathy, Indifference, Lack of enthusiasm, Weariness, Loathing, Distaste, Disinclination, Aversion

Zip
(Noun)
Synonyms: Energy, Drive, Gusto, Vitality, Fly, Shoot, Zoom, Vigor, Enthusiasm
Antonyms: Inertia, Apathy, Listlessness, Laziness, Sluggishness, Lethargy

LIST OF SYNONYMS AND ANTONYMS

The following synonyms and antonyms list are good, proficient-level words. They are an excellent place to improve your vocabulary building efforts.

SYNONYMS LIST

The following synonym list are presented alphabetically.

Word	Synonym	Synonym
A		
abandon	discard	vacate
accord	agree	grant
adversity	difficulty	misfortune
affluent	plentiful	rich
aggravate	annoy	infuriate
alleviate	lighten	mitigate
amenable	agreeable	favorable
anguish	distress	sorrow
apathetic	dispirited	lifeless
arrogant	disdainful	imperious
astonish	confound	overwhelm
atrocious	appalling	detestable
augment	add	enlarge
avoid	ignore	shun
awkward	graceless	inept

B

baffle	confuse	deceive
banal	common	plain
barren	desolate	sterile
berate	criticize	disapprove
betray	deceive	fool
bias	inclination	predisposition
bitter	acrid	sour
blend	combine	mix
bliss	happiness	joy
bluff	boast	feign
bold	daring	fearless
bonus	award	gift
bother	annoy	irritate
brief	concise	short
brilliant	clever	intelligent
brisk	fast	swift
budget	allot	plan

C

candid	honest	truthful
caricature	cartoon	imitation
casual	informal	natural
category	classification	division
cease	desist	stop
chaotic	disordered	messy
cherish	esteem	love
circumvent	avoid	go around
commemorate	celebrate	honor

compensate	balance	recompense
competent	able	capable
conceive	design	plan
confirmation	acknowledgement	proof
contradict	deny	oppose
contribution	donation	grant
courteous	polite	well-mannered
craving	desire	longing
credulous	confident	trustful

D

damp	moist	wet
dare	challenge	defy
decay	decline	rot
decent	honorable	pure
dense	filled	packed
designate	name	select
detain	hold	keep
disclose	announce	reveal
dogma	belief	view
durable	constant	lasting
dwindle	abate	diminish

E

eager	earnest	keen
eccentric	abnormal	idiosyncratic
elaborate	embellish	enhance
emanate	arise	radiate
embezzle	purloin	steal
eminent	distinguished	prominent

encourage	foster	induce
endure	last	persist
essential	cultured	learned
essential	basic	necessary
estimate	guess	predict
evaluate	appraise	judge
exhaust	deplete	empty
exhilarated	cheerful	zestful
explicit	definite	specific

F

fastidious	exacting	particular
federation	alliance	band
feeble	helpless	infirm
fervor	intensity	passion
feud	argument	dispute
filth	dirt	squalor
flatter	compliment	praise
fleet	nimble	swift
frivolous	inconsequential	trivial
frugal	prudent	saving
furious	angry	outraged

G

generous	benevolent	unselfish
genuine	actual	real
glare	gleam	glisten
gloomy	cheerless	dim
goad	provoke	badger
grasp	grab	hold
greed	avarice	longing

guarantee	assure	pledge
guile	cunning	deceit
gullible	credulous	unsuspicious

H

habitual	accustomed	regular
handicap	disability	disadvantage
harass	annoy	disturb
harmless	innocuous	inoffensive
harsh	hard	coarse
hasty	abrupt	hurried
haughty	arrogant	pretentious
humiliate	humble	shame
hygiene	cleanliness	sanitation
hypocrisy	duplicity	falseness

I

ideal	goal	perfection
idle	lazy	unoccupied
ignorant	stupid	unintelligent
illogical	incongruent	rambling
illustriou	eminent	famous
imitate	copy	reflect
immense	huge	mammoth
impartial	candid	impersonal
impatient	anxious	eager
implicate	accuse	insinuate
importune	beg	solicit
inadvertent	accidental	unintentional
indifferent	apathetic	disinterested

isolate	detach	quarantine

J

jargon	argot	slang
jovial	genial	merry
judge	estimate	referee
justification	excuse	reason
juvenile	adolescent	immature

K

keen	clever	observant

L

label	brand	classify
labor	toil	work
lead	direct	proceed
lean	slim	thin
leave	abandon	desert
liberal	copious	unrestrained
liberal	lenient	open-minded
limitation	boundary	constraint
lucid	clear	understandable
lucky	auspicious	fortunate

M

mad	furious	irate
manage	administer	control
manipulate	control	shape
marginal	borderline	limited

match	agree	correspond
maze	complexity	labyrinth
meditate	ponder	think
memorial	commemoration	monument
mention	allude	refer to
merge	blend	fuse

N

narrow	confined	restricted
nature	aspect	character
necessary	mandatory	requisite
negate	contradict	refute
negligent	careless	remiss
negotiate	bargain	deal
nice	affable	benign
noble	aristocratic	distinguished
novice	beginner	nonprofessional
nuisance	annoyance	offense

O

obedient	faithful	loyal
objection	disapproval	protest
obligatory	compulsory	required
observe	notice	watch
obvious	conspicuous	definite
offend	anger	irritate
offer	bid	proposal
omen	premonition	sign
omit	exclude	remove
opportune	advantageous	auspicious

P

pacify	appease	placate
pain	ache	discomfort
paramount	chief	leading
partisan	biased	dogmatic
passive	inactive	lethargic
pause	break	cease
permeate	diffuse	disseminate
perpetuate	endure	preserve
perplex	astonish	baffle
persecute	afflict	harass

R

radiate	effuse	emanate
radical	basic	fundamental
range	anger	furor
rank	arrange	classify
realize	accomplish	fulfill
recalcitrant	obstinate	stubborn
receptacle	container	repository
reconcile	atone	conciliate
regret	deplore	grieve
reliable	dependable	trustworthy

S

sanction	approval	permit
scope	aim	extent
section	division	portion

settle	adjust	compromise
shallow	superficial	trivial
shrewd	careful	calculating
significant	distinctive	important
slight	delicate	slender
spontaneous	impromptu	unplanned
spread	announce	broadcast
stabilize	balance	steady

T

tame	domesticate	subdue
tangle	intertwine	twist
temper	mood	nature
tendency	inclination	trend
term	cycle	duration
thrift	conservation	prudence
tough	aggressive	unyielding
transfer	convey	exchange
tumult	agitation	commotion
turbulent	disordered	violent

V

vain	boastful	inflated
valid	authorized	legitimate
variety	assortment	diversify
verify	authenticate	substantiate

ANTONYMS LIST

The following antonym list (opposites) are presented alphabetically.

Word	Antonym
A	
absence	presence
accept	refuse
accurate	inaccurate
advantage	disadvantage
alive	dead
always	never
ancient	modern
answer	question, query
approval	disapproval
approached	receded, departed
abundant	scarce
admit	deny
advance	retreat, retire
artificial	natural
arrival	departure
ascend	descend
attack	defense
attractive	repulsive
attention	inattention
asleep	awake
ally	enemy
agree	disagree

B

bad	good
backward	forward, onward
bend	straighten
beautiful	ugly
beginning	ending
below	above
bent	straight
big	small, little
blunt	sharp
better	worse
best	worst
blame	praise
bless	curse
bitter	sweet
borrow	lend
bravery	cowardice
build	destroy, demolish
bold	timid, meek
bright	dull
broad	narrow

C

clear	vague, cloudy
careful	rush, careless
calm	troubled
capable	incapable
captivity	freedom, liberty
cellar	attic

cheap	dear, expensive
close	distant
clever	stupid
cold	hot
combine	separate
clockwise	anti-clockwise
correct	incorrect
conceal	reveal
come	go
common	rare
comfort	discomfort
courage	cowardice
cruel	kind
courteous	discourteous, rude
cunning	simple

D

dainty	clumsy
danger	safety
dark	light
deep	shallow
decrease	increase
definite	indefinite
demand	supply
despair	hope
disappear	appear
disease	health
discourage	encourage
dismal	cheerful
doctor	patient

dry	wet
dull	clear, bright
dusk	dawn

E

early	late
easy	difficult
ebb	flow
East	West
economise	waste
encourage	discourage
entrance	exit
employer	employee
empty	full
excited	calm
end	beginning
expand	contract
expensive	inexpensive, cheap
export	import
exterior	interior
external	internal

F

fail	succeed
false	true
feeble	sturdy, strong, powerful
foolish	wise
fast	slow
few	many
famous	unknown

forelegs	hind legs
fat	thin
find	lose
first	last
freedom	captivity
fold	unfold
frequent	seldom
forget	remember
found	lost
fresh	stale
friend	enemy
fortunate	unfortunate
frank	secretive
full	empty

G

generous	mean
gentle	rough
gather	distribute
glad	sorry
gloomy	cheerful
giant	dwarf, pygmy
granted	refused
great	minute, small, little
guardian	ward
guest	host
guilty	innocent

H

happy	sad, miserable
hard	soft
harmful	harmless
hasten	dawdle
hate	love
healthy	unhealthy, ill, diseased
here	there
heavy	light
height	depth
hero	coward
hill	valley
horizontal	vertical
hinder	aid, help
honest	dishonest
humble	proud
hunger	thirst

I

imitation	genuine
immense	tiny, minute
imprison	free
include	exclude
increase	decrease
inhabited	uninhabited
inferior	superior
inside	outside
intelligent	unintelligent, stupid
inhale	exhale

interior	exterior, outside
interesting	uninteresting, dull
internal	external
intentional	accidental

J

join	separate
junior	senior
justice	injustice

K

king	subject
knowledge	ignorance

L

laugh	cry
lawful	unlawful
lazy	industrious, energetic
land	sea
landlord	tenant
large	little, small
last	first
lawyer	client

N

night	day
noisy	quiet
North	South

O

obedient	disobedient
odd	even
offer	refuse
open	shut
optimist	pessimist
out	in

P

parent	child
past	present
patient	impatient
peace	war
permanent	temporary
please	displease
plentiful	scarce
poetry	prose
possible	impossible
poverty	wealth
powerful	feeble, weak
polite	impolite, rude
private	public
prudent	imprudent
pretty	unsightly, ugly
pure	impure

Q

qualified	unqualified

R

rapid	slow
regularly	irregularly
rich	poor
right	wrong, left
rigid	pliable, soft
rough	smooth

S

satisfactory	unsatisfactory
security	insecurity
scatter	collect
serious	trivial
second-hand	new
sense	nonsense
shopkeeper	customer
singular	plural
simple	complicated
slim	thick, stout
solid	liquid
sober	drunk
speaker	listener
sour	sweet
sorrow	joy
sow	reap
stand	lie
straight	crooked
strong	weak
success	failure
sunny	cloudy

T

take	give
tall	short
tame	wild
teacher	pupil
thick	thin
tight	slack, loose
top	bottom
transparent	opaque
truth	untruth, lie

U

up	down

V

vacant	occupied
valuable	valueless
victory	defeat
virtue	vice
visible	invisible
voluntary	compulsory
vowel	consonant

W

wax	wane
wisdom	folly
within	without